POGBA

About the authors

Luca Caioli is the bestselling author of *Messi, Ronaldo* and *Neymar*. A renowned Italian sports journalist, he lives in Spain.

Cyril Collot is a French journalist. He is the author of several books about the French national football team and Olympique Lyonnais. Nowadays he works for the OLTV channel, where he has directed several documentaries about football.

POGBA

2018 Edition

LUCA CAIOLI
&
CYRIL COLLOT

ICON

Published in the UK in 2017
by Icon Books Ltd, Omnibus Business Centre,
39–41 North Road, London N7 9DP
email: info@iconbooks.com
www.iconbooks.com

Sold in the UK, Europe and Asia
by Faber & Faber Ltd, Bloomsbury House,
74–77 Great Russell Street,
London WC1B 3DA or their agents

Distributed in the UK, Europe and Asia
by Grantham Book Services, Trent Road, Grantham NG31 7XQ

Distributed in the USA
by Publishers Group West,
1700 Fourth Street, Berkeley, CA 94710

Distributed in Australia and New Zealand
by Allen & Unwin Pty Ltd,
PO Box 8500, 83 Alexander Street,
Crows Nest, NSW 2065

Distributed in South Africa
by Jonathan Ball, Office B4, The District,
41 Sir Lowry Road, Woodstock 7925

Distributed in India by Penguin Books India,
7th Floor, Infinity Tower – C, DLF Cyber City,
Gurgaon 122002, Haryana

Distributed in Canada by Publishers Group Canada,
76 Stafford Street, Unit 300
Toronto, Ontario M6J 2S1

ISBN: 978-178578-239-8

Typeset in New Baskerville by Marie Doherty

Printed and bound in the UK
by Clays Ltd, St Ives plc

Contents

Chapter 1
Son of Yeo Moriba and Fassou Antoine

The quickest way to trace the origins of the Pogba family is to open an atlas. Put your finger on the African continent; allow it to move west, passing Morocco, Mauritania and finally landing on the Republic of Guinea. This will save you a tiring eight hour flight from Paris to Conakry. However, this virtual journey is far from over. Use your index finger to make an arc from left to right, from the Guinean capital of almost three and a half million inhabitants, turn your back on the Atlantic Ocean to fly over the cities of Kindia and Mamou, carefully follow the borders with Sierra Leone and Liberia before reaching Guéckédou, and bring your journey to an end in Nzérékoré. In no time at all, you have travelled almost a thousand extra kilometres without too much trouble. There are no internal flights or railways across the country from west to east. To get there you must make it along hundreds of kilometres of red dirt tracks by 4×4, avoiding the ruts often concealed by the dust that flies up as bush taxis and overloaded trucks speed past. You will also need to cross towns that may not necessarily appear on your map: Banian, Kissidougou, Macenta and Sérédou.

When you get to Nzérékoré, the country's third biggest town, the worst is yet to come — around 40 kilometres of roads deemed unsafe, dangerous and often blocked by heavy flooding during the rainy season. Finally, after another hour and a half, a small village comes into view at the end of the road, a sort of balcony overlooking the rainforest.

Fassou Antoine Pogba Hébélamou was born here, in the heart of Forested Guinea, on 27 March 1938. It was in Péla that Paul's father grew up.

In this landscape at the edge of the world that was hit hard by the Ebola virus between 2013 and 2015 (11,300 deaths in West Africa). Right in the middle of the Mount Nimba nature reserve, not far from the Ziama Massif, home to a formidable variety of flora and fauna, where more than two hundred species, such as duikers (small deer), the favourite meal of lions and leopards, abound. 'It's a typical African bush village. It consists of a centre with houses scattered all around. The inhabitants work in the fields; they are known in the region as "*Forestiers*"', says Alban Traquet, the only European journalist to have made the real-life journey to Péla for a report on the origins of the Pogba family for *L'Équipe* in March 2017. 'It's a no man's land, one of the most remote and poorest places in the country. Nor is it a region spared from hardship: in addition to the ravages of Ebola, it is almost completely cut off from the outside world for eight months a year due to heavy rains.'

Although the official language is French, Guinea is home to almost twenty dialects. Diakhanké, Malinké and Susu are the most widely spoken. In Péla they speak Guerzé, also known as Kpelle. This language, which binds the village's 5,600 inhabitants, is shared with their close neighbours in Liberia and spoken throughout the south of Guinea, particularly in the region of the Nzérékoré prefecture. It is from this dialect that one of the most famous surnames of the 21st century comes: 'Pogba is not their real family name,' reveals Alban Traquet. 'They were originally known as "Hébélamou". The name "Pogba" was attributed to Paul's grandfather because he was particularly influential in the village. In the Guerzé language it means "reverential son", or someone who is respected and listened to by his family. Since then, the whole family has kept the name.'

Fassou Antoine first arrived in Paris in the mid-1960s, when he was in his thirties. Guinea was undergoing drastic upheaval at the time. A French colony since 1891, it obtained its independence in October 1958 after opposing the referendum announced by General Charles de Gaulle, who wanted the country to be part of a new French Community. The response was scathing: in the following month, France began its withdrawal from the country, leaving the Guineans deprived of military and financial aid, as well as many civil servants, including teachers, doctors and nurses. It was at this time that Fassou Antoine packed his bags to settle in the Paris region, where he began a career in telecommunications, before becoming a teacher at a technical high school. The rather poised and discreet young man was passionate about the round ball. This passion had developed at an early age, and stayed with him over the years. He was a keen fan of the 'Syli', the Guinean national team, and, since arriving in France, he had been involved in the founding of the Africa Star de Paris football club, which brought the local Guinean community together until 1990.

The remoteness and inaccessibility of Péla meant that visits home to his childhood village were rare. He did return in the late 1980s, however, when he spent time with his younger brother Badjopé and one of his sisters, Kébé: 'God had not blessed my brother Fassou with children. He was living in France and was fifty, so he returned home to sacrifice a ram in the hope of finding fertility,' Kébé told the journalist

Alban Traquet when he visited the village. 'He then left again for Conakry in search of a romantic relationship.'

This sacrificial ceremony therefore marked the starting point for the meeting between the Christian, Fassou Antoine and the future mother of Paul Pogba, a Muslim woman in her twenties named Yeo Moriba. Like her future husband, she was from Forested Guinea, but from the village of Mabossou, located about 100 kilometres north of Péla. The daughter of a civil servant, she came from a family of well-known figures: her great uncle, Louis Lansana Beavogui was the Prime Minister of Guinea between 1972 and 1984 and even temporarily occupied the position of head of state after the death of the illustrious Sékou Touré, but he was quickly overthrown and imprisoned following a military coup. There was also, to a lesser extent, her cousin, Riva Touré, who had had a brief career as a footballer in Guinea and worn the prestigious shirt of AS Kaloum Star. The Conakry club had done well for itself by winning the national league a dozen times. Yeo Moriba, a cheerful and determined young woman, also had a soft spot for the country's number one sport, which she practised diligently. She was doing well for herself and was on the point of being named captain of the national women's team.

Despite the age difference, the couple had a number of things in common thanks to their passion for football and background in Forested Guinea. This was only the beginning, Yeo was soon expecting twins! The ram sacrifice had not been in vain. Yeo Moriba gave birth to two beautiful boys, Florentin and Mathias, on 19 August 1990. The small family would spend two years in the port city of Conakry before leaving the Guinean capital to settle permanently in France, about 30 kilometres to the south-east of Paris, in Roissy-en-Brie.

A former hunting ground with 150 hectares of forest that it shared with the neighbouring town of Torcy, the commune in Seine-et-Marne was undergoing profound change and development. The census takers had their work cut out over twenty years: the population had risen from 500 to almost 20,000 inhabitants in 1992. In other words, the wheat fields had given way to buildings of all kinds by the time the couple and their two children took possession of an apartment in the Le Bois-Briard development in a peaceful area to the north-east of the city. The family grew a year later thanks to the arrival of a third son: Paul Labile Pogba, who was born on 15 March 1993. Like all local children, he came into the world at the maternity unit in Lagny-sur-Marne hospital, about ten kilometres from his home.

Back in Guinea, the news of the birth of a new member of the Pogba family spread very quickly. Rosine, one of the maternal aunts who had also settled in the capital, would be one of the first to visit the little miracle. She remembers this of her stay in France: 'The twins were there and Paul was tiny. He was six months old. The day I arrived, I held him in my arms and put some big sunglasses on him for a photo,' she says, showing an image of her giving a bottle to the newest member of the family, who is all smiles. 'I can say that he was born with success and that he had it in his blood. This was the blessing I gave to his mother.'

In the villages of Mabossou and Péla, Paul would be seen only in snapshots sent from France. Although Yeo Moriba kept close ties with her country, where she now owns a luxury house given to her by her youngest son in the Kipé neighbourhood of Conakry, his father, Fassou Antoine, gradually became more distant. He never returned to his native village after the famous ram sacrifice in 1989 and was never able to officially introduce his three sons: 'But that did not stop the creation of a link and in Péla a huge portrait of Paul has been painted in the town hall,' reports Alban Traquet. 'It's a way of thanking him for his many gifts. He has given the village a sound system, a generator and a flat screen for the video club. He also funded the sending of a hundred 50 kg bags of rice to help the needy. He and his brothers sent two sets of FC Pogba printed shirts for the young people of the village in the colours of Manchester United and AS Saint-Étienne, where Florentin plays.'

Of course, they all hope to see Paul come to the village of Péla in the flesh one day and not only just to make it as far as the capital Conakry, as he did in 2011. This one visit to the country of his ancestors nevertheless left its mark on him. He will never forget what he saw on the streets of the capital. This journey of initiation carried out in the year he turned eighteen gave him a close-up view of suffering and helped him understand how lucky he had been. It also taught him to share and measure his happiness. 'Over there, they laugh, they play football and they have nothing, but they seem happier than we do, Europeans who have everything,' he would say in the summer of 2016. 'You're black, they're black but they know you're not from there. All that helped me grow.'

In the mid-1990s, one event marked the childhood of Paul Pogba. At that time, he was still far from imagining what awaited him. Too young to see into his future. Too young to remember his family's heartbreak. When he was only two years old, his parents decided to separate. Fassou Antoine kept the apartment at Le Bois-Briard. Yeo Moriba moved a little further away but still in the town of Roissy-en-Brie. With her three children by her side, she went to live in the neighbourhood known as La Renardière.

Chapter 2

Football, Ping Pong and the City Stade

It was always the same. Her children never knew when to stop. Yeo Moriba had to raise her voice: 'Hey, boys! It's time to come in! Hurry up, it's dark and you've got to go to bed,' she shouted from her window on the twelfth floor of the tall white tower, using her deep, strident voice to make herself heard through the branches of the large pine trees that concealed the playground a hundred metres or so below. If she had not intervened that night, her three sons would have kept on playing until dawn. Florentin, Mathias and Paul eventually finished their match, picked up their ball and ran up alleyway no. 13 at the Résidence La Renardière.

Paul was seven years old; Mathias and Florentin were ten. The City Stade had just been built at the end of the playground, along the railway track. It quickly became a rallying point for all the local kids. Since the 1970s, La Renardière had been home to fourteen blocks of varying sizes. Several buildings are scattered across the large landscaped estate among four large towers with up to thirteen floors. It was in one of those, the closest to Avenue Auguste Renoir, that Yeo Moriba had settled with her family five years earlier.

In the modest uncluttered apartment, she brought up her three sons and two nieces on her own: 'They were the daughters of her big sister,' explained a close friend of the family. 'They were called Marie-Yvette and Poupette. They're in their thirties now. One lives in England and the other in the south of Paris. They played the role of big sisters and sometimes mothers to the boys, preparing meals for them or taking Paul to the Pommier Picard School across the street.'

To be able to provide for everyone, Yeo Moriba took on several jobs: she worked as a chambermaid in a hotel, a cashier at a supermarket and an employee at an aid association for the handicapped. She struggled to ensure that her children would not go without: 'I made a lot of sacrifices. I worked morning and night to support them, so they wouldn't be picked on by their schoolmates, would be happy and could go on holiday,' she tells the journalists who come to interview her in her new well-to-do apartment in Bussy-Saint-Georges (about 30 kilometres from Roissy-en-Brie), in which the living room looks more like a museum with its carefully arranged newspaper clippings and photos.

The boys were inseparable. Paul could always be found with the twins. 'They were like the Three Musketeers. The twins really mollycoddled their younger brother. They were always as thick as thieves,' explains Henri, a long-time resident of the neighbourhood who we meet while crossing the car park. Paul had a strong character and was a real showman. He liked to dance, sing and play the clown. He soon came up with nicknames for the whole family. Starting with himself. He christened himself '*La Pioche*' (The Pickaxe). 'There was an Ivorian actor in a TV series, Gohou Michel, who always said "*La Pioche, il va piocher le village*" [The Pickaxe, he's going to use his pickaxe in the village], '*Pogby La Pioche.*' I liked it so even my mother started calling me "*La Pioche*",' Paul said in 2016. Next came the turn of his two brothers: Florentin, the craziest, would be 'Red Bull in his blood,' then

'*Flo Zer*' and then just '*Le Zer*.' Mathias, who 'had a back like a gorilla', would be simply '*Le Dos*': *The Back*.

Le Zer, *Le Dos* and *La Pioche* soon carved out a reputation for themselves in the neighbourhood. At the end of the school day, they would take possession of the small pitch and entertain themselves while perfecting their technique to impress their friends: keepie uppies with their left foot, right foot, and head, dribbling and firing shots towards the goal. Champions in the making!

At the City Stade, where the handrails have been repainted bright red and grey and the artificial pitch replaced by concrete, they now play both basketball and football. Surrounded by a dozen kids shouting and running in all directions, two local teenagers, Bryan and Kévin are quietly shooting hoops to the rhythm of the beats emanating from a small speaker. They know the Pogbas by reputation. One of the two kids points to a large white wall that had been home to a huge portrait of the future French international for more than a year: 'It was painted by the local kids but then covered up. But there's still a poster of Paul on the landing of his old apartment. Proof that he was here.'

However, our two NBA aficionados know nothing of the football tournaments that saw the local kids face off during the school holidays in the early 2000s. Matches at the social centres saw players from La Renardière challenge other residences such as '50 Arpents', 'Bois-Briard' and 'La Pierrerie'. 'Games were held over two legs, home and away,' explains Yoann, in his thirties, once a young footballing hopeful now working as a chauffeur. 'You should have seen the level! The winner was the first to ten. In the early days, Paul waited quietly behind the handrail, watching his brothers intently.'

But he would not remain a spectator at these five-a-sides for long. His brothers soon threw him in at the deep end: the

'City' would be his first training academy. 'We were happy he wanted to play with us and not mess about with the kids his own age,' explain his two brothers. 'It helped give him character.'

The three Pogbas were given offensive positions. Mathias and Florentin, also nicknamed the Derrick brothers after the cartoon *Captain Tsubasa*, played on the wings. Paul was put in the central midfield. No prisoners were taken in this rough street football; the boys played right up against the walls and would even hit each other during one-on-one's. Paul was often knocked to the ground. Whenever a tear began to appear in the corner of his eye, he was immediately called to order: 'Stop crying and play!' his brothers commanded. As the matches went on, he began to toughen up. He resisted better, learned to fight his own corner, became stronger and made progress.

The kid had character alright, as well as a marked taste for competition, something it was said he got from his father, Fassou Antoine. He did not like to lose and was lucky because La Renardière often came out the winner of these local matches. But it was not just about football. Whenever he lost at cards at home or at the PlayStation, he would get himself into a real state. He wanted to play over and over again to compete with his brothers. It was the same when he discovered table tennis, thanks to Florentin and Mathias. Luckily, the club was just five minutes' walk from the residence. At the time there was even a shortcut across waste ground to avoid Avenue Eugène Delacroix.

The Salle Jacques Rossignol, built from beige and blue sheet metal, is set back from the road, just behind a small dirt car park. At the time, the US Roissy Table Tennis club had just taken over the space left vacant by a bowls club. It was the perfect spot to line up almost a dozen tables with the space behind them to allow the players to move around comfortably. In 1999, Patrick Sembla, a former professional and the life and soul of the club where he has been coaching for more than twenty years, remembers the arrival of the Pogba twins, followed very quickly by the youngest member of the family: 'They were always accompanied by their two big "sisters", who would drop them off in the late afternoon and then collect them around 8.30pm. Paulo, as I nicknamed him, wanted to do everything Mathias and Florentin did. He was a smart kid. A nice kid, always happy and motivated. He tried to copy his brothers in every way. He tried and tried again and again until he got there. He was extremely gifted and clearly had the mental, physical and tactical ability to succeed. He would learn in three minutes what it took others a year to assimilate. He had all the qualities to become a champion, in table tennis or in any other sport, for that matter.'

In table tennis, it would be the twins who would win the prizes, however. Florentin became champion of Seine-et-Marne and Île-de-France. Mathias did even better and became French Under-11 champion. 'They were so much better than everyone else that they shared out the wins and were happy to knock balls around in the finals,' explains Sembla. 'Sometimes one would win and then the next time the other. They had this determination to be the best, whatever the sport. You could feel their will to win.' One of Paul's best memories is of a tournament in Roissy-en-Brie where he was playing in a higher age category and could play against the rest of the family for once. Wearing the light blue shirt of US Roissy TT, the Pogbas pulled off an incredible family victory: 'Flo 1st, Mathias 2nd and Paulo 3rd.' Paul can only have been seven or eight but he was already ranked among the three best table tennis players in Seine-et-Marne in the Under-11 age group.

Despite his promise, Paul eventually said goodbye to table tennis aged nine: 'His brothers had just been selected among the best young table tennis hopefuls in Île-de-France and Paul probably didn't want to carry on playing the sport on his own in Roissy. Florentin and Mathias wanted to go as far as they could in table tennis but in the end it became tough for them because they also had ambitions in football. Within a year they had all stopped,' says a regretful Patrick Sembla, who keeps several photos of the Pogba brothers on his phone as a souvenir. In one of these, the coach is flanked by the twins on the day Mathias won the title of French champion. In another, Paul is wearing a navy and white t-shirt at the front of a group of about twenty kids. As always, his brothers are not far away, just behind him wearing the club shirt. 'I've got other ones but I prefer to keep them for myself. Paul is so concerned about his look and appearance that he would hate me if I made them public.'

In the end, Paul decided to devote himself entirely to his favourite sport but presumably has no regrets about the time he spent at US Roissy Table Tennis: 'Table tennis is a sport that requires a lot of concentration. If you get upset you lose your match. That helps me a lot today.' The insatiable competitor surrendered his weapons without ever managing to beat Mathias or Florentin. They were too good for him but were still careful to look after their little brother: 'Back then, whenever they received a cheque or some money for winning a tournament, they bought me a pair of shoes. I always told them I would pay them back.'

Chapter 3

RLS (Roissy-la-Source)

It is a Wednesday like any other at the Stade Paul-Bessuard. And yet as soon as you go through the little gate, for some strange reason it feels like the first weekend of the summer holidays. At the USR, the Union Sportive de Roissy, kids are running back and forth like cars on the A7 Autoroute du Soleil from Paris to the beaches of the south during the summer exodus. The hustle and bustle is constant, sometimes causing traffic jams in the narrow alleyway that borders the new artificial pitch and runs alongside the dressing rooms and office. Some of the kids greet each other with a tap of the fist and a '*Check mon pote*', others run after each other shouting 'You can't catch me!' while others still chat about their morning at school. One takes refuge in the secretary's office to read a love letter away from prying eyes. He is quickly chased out by the secretary herself, Martine: 'Shoo, you can't be in here!' He is swallowed up by the influx of young footballers with a colourful mix of shirts and origins who give this town in Seine-et-Marne its character. A little black kid wearing a Real Madrid shirt returns to his mother, who is armed with a large pushchair in which his little sister is taking a nap. 'Say goodbye and don't forget to ask your coach why you didn't play last weekend!' The little boy does as he is told and runs off, teasing another kid who is not allowed a snack during Ramadan as he goes. 'Do you want some?' he mocks a teammate wearing full PSG strip while waving a piece of cake under his nose. A few yards away, the instructors do not bat an eyelid. They are too busy carrying out a head count and dishing out invitations to play in matches that weekend, like sweets. The wind catches these invitations as they fly away over the offices while the kids look on with amusement. Their run comes to an end on the other side beneath the covered stand that overlooks the main pitch. On Wednesdays its turf is used to teach the youngest children the basics. You could spend hours there just admiring the show. A tall, slender black man with a fine white goatee beard and an Olympique Lyonnais cap is fussing around a dozen children who cannot be more than five at most. Some of them are wearing the club's socks, recognisable by their wide blue and white stripes. They are all wearing bibs that are far too large for them. They are so small and light the ball seems to weigh them down like an anvil. They struggle to move, so much so that their instructor is constantly interrupting them and gesturing with his arms. 'The greens are going that way. Why are you shooting in this direction?' a man in his fifties asks a nervous little blond boy. A few seconds later, he restarts the game: 'Play!' A mother takes advantage of the interruption to retie her son's laces.

The instructor cuts such an imposing figure that it is hard to take your eyes off him. He dispenses so much good advice that he could be a wise village elder: authoritarian when necessary but still keeping an eye out for the slightest graze or mishap. It is not surprising that he knows how to deal with the kids. Mamadou Diouf has been training coaches in Île-de-France and the district for more than twenty years. He is also the technical manager of the football school: 'US Roissy is a family club,' he explains after his session. '95 per cent of our players live in the town. There's a strong social cohesion here. In 2010, we opened the club up to children aged four because that allowed us to better target the kids and to teach them ball control more easily. This is reflected in their progress. For example, in the Under-9 category our boys are already capable of 30 keepie uppies with both feet and fifteen with their heads. That bears fruit and now we're almost a victim of our success. Even more so when people find out that Paul Pogba came through here. We have almost 550 players. You can't imagine how many want to be like him and copy his haircut! It's great marketing for the club! Some parents think if they sign their kid up with us they'll be just as successful.' It is not hard to imagine the scene: proud fathers hoping that one day their son's shirt will be carefully folded in a frame hanging on the wall of the little locked office that serves as a makeshift museum for US Roissy. Hanging next to the red and white PSV Eindhoven shirt printed with the number 2 of Nicolas Isimat-Mirin and relics of all three Pogba brothers. A light blue shirt with the unlikely number 99 that belonged to Mathias, a green AS Saint-Étienne jersey with Florentin's number 19, and the black and white shirt worn by Paul when he made his debut for Juventus. The shirt is genuine and signed. The local star even took the trouble to write a message in red felt tip pen across the white printing of his number 6: 'To my first dream club, Roissy-en-Brie.'

Paul joined the club in September 1999. He was following in the footsteps of his two brothers, just as he had done with table tennis. The immaculate artificial pitch funded by the town council did not yet exist. The kids played on a 'red pitch' as it is known here, a dirt pitch at the end of the complex that has now fallen into disuse. Sambou Tati was his first coach. Like his protégé he has come a long way. 'I've been through practically everything at US Roissy. I started playing when I was thirteen, then I became a director, coach and I've been president for a few years now. I can't even tell you how long it's been, it's gone so quickly,' says the 48 year old, who looks a good ten years younger. 'I was 30 when I coached Paul's generation for the first time. I got to know him through his two brothers who were at the club and showed a lot of promise. I also had the opportunity to meet him at the social clubs because I was a youth worker. He was a kid like any other, except you could already see how gifted he was. When he played on the neighbourhood pitches, he scored goal after goal.'

Of course, the baby of the family had plenty of opportunity to follow in his brothers' footsteps. The football stadium was very close to La Renardière. It took less than ten minutes to walk there past the cemetery, where the boules players gather, and out onto Rue Yitzhak Rabin, a stone's throw from the sports complex.

Fassou Antoine had given his approval. The boys' father took the activity very seriously, in fact. He did not wait for his youngest son to enrol at the club before putting him through his paces. Whenever the children came to visit, he would give them special sessions on a small dirt pitch near his apartment in Le Bois-Briard. He had them work on their technique and gave them plenty of tips. Over and over, he would tell the three brothers: 'You have to learn to win whatever the circumstances.' He told Paul to take the example set by his older brothers, to copy what they did and show the same will to win on the pitch. *La Pioche* listened to his father's recommendations, which he intended to put into practice in September 1999 when he first played in a US Roissy shirt.

How did his first training session go? 'He was impressive,' remembers Sambou Tati, better known at the club by the nickname 'Bijou' (jewel or gem). 'Paul likes to say that he scored two or three goals that day. To be frank, I don't remember, and it's difficult to say because at that age the goals are made from cones without a crossbar. It's not easy to work out whether the ball has flown over the top or not. One thing for sure is that he had no fear. He wanted to dribble all the time, keep the ball and shoot from anywhere on the pitch. He was a bit selfish, but he was only six years old. It was just the beginning, the "source" as he likes to remember it.'

RLS, Roissy-la-Source: the expression was invented by a group of rappers who created a buzz in Roissy in the 1990s and 2000s. Such as Ousmane Traoré, who has since joined the Canadian hip hop group Dubmatique, and the local Maramata collective: 'RLS is something Paul will talk about all his life,' says Tati. 'For him, the source is a tribute to this town where he knows he is loved and where he feels at home, to his neighbourhood La Renardière, where he spent so many wonderful years surrounded by his family and friends, and to our club, where he started out and grew. Roissy-la-Source is also Paul Pogba. He has now inspired generations of players in turn and is the pride of our club. The kids dream of having the same destiny and to us he will always be a US Roissy player.'

Chapter 4
The Stadium of Dreams

It is a photo that marks a moment in history. It dates from 6 September 2003. There is nothing particularly extraordinary about it. It shows twelve children in red and blue club tracksuits and a youthful looking coach. It was taken in the square at Saint-Denis, just outside the Stade de France. There is nothing particularly unusual about that either because young teams from the Paris region are often invited to attend matches played by the Bleus, and Roissy is only about twenty minutes from the huge stadium that brought so much joy to France at the 1998 World Cup final. The Bleus were at home to Cyprus that evening in a qualifying game for Euro 2004 to be played the following summer in Portugal. An injured Zidane had been ruled out but there were still plenty of top-quality players on show. A fine bunch of former world champions: Barthez, Thuram, Desailly, Lizarazu, Vieira, Pires and the duo of Henry and Trezeguet, who would score three of the five goals during the stroll against the Cypriots.

It was a much-anticipated evening for the Under-11s from US Roissy. Some had had trouble sleeping since their coach, Aziz Keftouna, had told them the news. For most of them it would be the first time they would see the France team. Most importantly they would have the opportunity to show what they could do in two matches as a curtain-raiser for the Bleus. 'It was a dream come true,' confirms Doudou Konte, one of Paul's closest friends. 'We were all super excited. Our club had been invited in recognition of its good results. We had the chance to visit the dressing rooms and were even given red outfits printed with the France team sponsor, which Paul kept I think.'

'It really is an amazing memory,' says Habib Bouacida, who was in Paul's class throughout at Roissy, from the Under-7s to the Under-13s. 'The France team players were just a few metres away from us watching our match. It was unreal! We came out of it pretty well with a draw and a win against US Créteil and FC Metz. After the match, we had our photo taken with Fabien Barthez and Djibril Cissé. It made such an impression on us.'

In 2003, Habib, Doudou, Paul and the others shared the same dream of becoming professional footballers. This objective fed into their daily lives and influenced every conversation they had. 'We all wanted to succeed,' confirms Doudou Konte, a defensive midfielder in the French fifth division with a local club, US Sénart-Moissy. 'I loved Ronaldo, and Paul and I were both big Ronaldinho fans. He would watch videos of his matches and try to copy everything he did on the pitch.'

The small group that had been playing together for four or five years was particularly competitive and more tight-knit than ever: 'We came from different parts of Roissy. Some were from La Renardière, others from the Zones, the Grands-Champs or near the station. I lived in 50 Arpents,' explains Doudou. 'Football brought us together and we quickly became friends. There was a great atmosphere in the team despite our very different characters. There were those who were full of energy, like Habib, Nasser and our captain, Nabil. Our goalkeeper, Ounoussou Timera, was nicknamed "The Mute" and Paul was "The Grouch" or "Mr Grumpy".' There was also 'The Spaniard', Asier Azcarreta, who went to live in Madrid but remembers the tough character of his former teammate: 'I played with him for five years and it was incredible how he refused to lose. If we did lose he would cry. On the other hand, Paul was always the last to leave training. He would practise things over and over again until he got them.'

An incredible will to win, supreme self-confidence and most importantly pure talent. His former teammates have anecdotes in spades when it comes to *La Pioche*'s exploits in the red and blue shirt.

Doudou Konte: 'He could easily dribble past three or four players in the same move. If the opposition scored a goal, he would take the ball and commit until he equalised.'

Timera Ounoussou: 'Before joining the club I had a neighbour who played at US Roissy and wouldn't stop telling me about this kid called Paul. He would say: "You'll see. He's so good!" When I had my first training session with the Under-10s, I didn't need to ask the others what his name was. I knew he was the famous Paul. He caught my eye immediately. He already had a right and a left foot. He was a technical leader and most importantly had a winner's mentality. I said to myself that day: "He'll go far."'

Asier Azcarreta: 'I remember a tournament when he was voted best player, as was often the case. But that time there were some fantastic teams, like PSG, Olympique Marseille and some Spanish clubs. Our coach's tactics were simple. Before the match he told us: "Pass the ball to Pogba, he'll make the difference!"'

From the Under-10s onwards, Paul was clearly a cut above his teammates. His successive coaches, Mamadou Magassa (nicknamed 'Papis'), Aziz Keftouna, his mentor, and Bilel Diallo, the technical director, were unanimous in their praise of his incredible potential. His mother was kept updated by her cousin, Riva Touré, the former professional back in Guinea, who now also lived in Roissy-en-Brie and even worked at the club. He followed the kid closely, giving him tips and insisting Yeo Moriba come to watch him play to see how impressive he really was. 'We had a fantastic generation,' remembers Papis Magassa. 'Players such as Doudou, Habib, Nabil and our keeper, Ounoussou, who now plays in the fourth division. We also had a striker in the team, Christopher Mve Bekale, who scored goal after goal. But in this excellent group, Paul was the individual who often tipped the match in our direction.'

The problem was that he was often punished, something that became more and more frequent when he left the Pommier Picard primary school to join the Eugène Delacroix middle school just 200 metres further away from home. The Collège Eugène Delacroix is two white buildings in the middle of a green space and a residential area, linked to the Georges Chanu gym where kids from Year 7 to Year 10 attend sports classes during the week. 'School? Let's just say that it wasn't his thing and he messed about like everyone does,' admits Doudou Konte, with a hint of a smile that speaks volumes about anecdotes he would rather keep to himself. Paul's mother is uncompromising for the TV cameras, however: 'He was a total nightmare at school. He was lively. He would tease his friends and the girls in his class because he was so high-spirited.' Despite being a little embarrassed, Paul can only confirm: 'It's true, I was a real chatterbox. I couldn't keep still. I had ants in my pants.'

Paul's attitude was not to Fassou Antoine's liking. His father, a teacher, struggled increasingly seeing his children neglect their studies for thoughts only of football. 'Sometimes, he didn't turn up at training so we would call his mum to make sure he was okay. In the end it would turn out that his father had punished him. He was tough but fair with him. Paul could cry for hours, but he would never go back on his decision.'

Except once perhaps, when faced with an insistent Papis Magassa: 'We were supposed to play the final of the Under-12 Seine-et-Marne cup and I had strengthened the team with some of the oldest kids eligible. Paul was one of those. But the day before I received a phone call from his father, who told me: "He's been punished, he won't be coming tomorrow!"

'I replied: "But you can't do that! Tomorrow is the most important match of the year. Punish him next week."

'But he wouldn't budge: "No, he has to be punished tomorrow!"

'So I told him: "Listen, I'm coming over to your house. I'm going to make him work, help him with his homework, but please don't punish him tomorrow."'

In the end, Paul did turn up that Saturday for the famous final played in the neighbouring town of Chelles. US Roissy even won the trophy. After a 1–0 win, followed by a draw, Papis Magassa's players beat Lognes 2–0. In this decisive match, Paul had a magnificent free kick disallowed: 'It was a stunning goal that skimmed the underside of the crossbar, but the referee was the only one who didn't see the ball cross the line,' remembers his coach.

The 2005–06 season was looming. His seventh and last at the club. In the Under-13 category, Paul was reunited with his first coach, Sambou Tati; despite being considered 'a big brother' by the three Pogbas, he would not spare the baby of the family. 'I put him in as playmaker. I spent my time telling him to play more simply and to stop showboating but he didn't listen to me. So I gave him an ear bashing at half time: "Paul, you're not Ronaldinho, you're crap, you're not the star in this team, you're bringing nothing." He started crying, but as soon as the second half kicked off, he massacred everyone.'

US Roissy finished third in its league. Paul even made several appearances for the Under-15s. Scouts from professional clubs began hanging around the pitches but Fassou Antoine was not ready to hear talk of leaving Roissy just yet. Because of his academic results, his son had just failed the entrance exam for the INF Clairefontaine, the pre-training academy for the best footballers in Île-de-France. It was not surprising. Paul was getting ready to repeat Year 8. 'The end of the season was tricky,' recalls Papis Magassa. 'He was defeated and disappointed by these early failures. But we weren't worried. Given his potential, he just needed time to digest them and we were in no doubt that he would soon bounce back.'

Chapter 5

Growing up in Torcy

The US Torcy Paris-Val-de-Marne website includes a photo gallery of players who have passed through the club and gone on to become professional footballers. It includes around thirty faces and, when you click on the images, several of them look familiar. They are Yohann Pelé, the Olympique Marseille goalkeeper, Mourad Meghni, a midfielder in Italy with Bologna and then Lazio, and the Mali international Samba Diakité, who spent time in the English league between 2012 and 2014 with Queens Park Rangers and Watford. They are nearly all there and 'with all these players we could practically pick a team that would sit happily in the middle of the French first division table!' claims Jean-Pierre Damont, in charge of the club between 1992 and 2010. You could take the former president at his word were this family album not missing its most famous member: Paul Pogba.

La Pioche did not hang around at US Torcy. He only played one season between July 2006 and June 2007. How did his first transfer to this neighbouring town of just over 20,000 inhabitants come about? On good terms, according to the explanation given by Sambou Touati: 'After such a good season, he couldn't stay with us. He was too good for Roissy, so I advised him to join Torcy. It wasn't too far from home for him, about ten kilometres, and he could continue to progress there by playing in a better league with a team that was more competitive. Even though some of the instructors and directors here didn't necessarily agree with me, I picked up the phone and contacted the neighbouring club.'

Stéphane Albe, the coach at Torcy, was not surprised by the call; he had already heard of Paul Pogba. The two clubs crossed paths throughout the year, both in the league and at other tournaments. Paul's arrival had been in the pipeline for some time: 'Our clubs had always had a good relationship and we knew about Paul's potential,' says the 45-year-old. 'It had been agreed with the directors at Roissy that he would stay with them while he was still playing on a smaller pitch and would only come to us when he had moved on to eleven-a-side football. That was the case that season with our Under-14 team, who played at the highest regional level.'

Those who were less enthusiastic about the move to their Seine-et-Marne rivals were Paul's long-standing friends, Doudou in particular: 'When he went to Torcy, we joked with him that he was a traitor. We had played together forever and it was a bit like the end of an adventure. But we understood his choice and didn't insist.'

'It was a real opportunity for him,' confirms Ounoussou, the goalkeeper, also recruited by Torcy a few years later. 'He was going to have the chance to play four divisions above us, something he shouldn't have missed out on. It was the perfect springboard for him.'

Although US Torcy did not have the prestige of a professional club, it was undoubtedly a key player in youth football in the Paris region. A sort of antechamber for the training academies, a rite of passage coveted by those who had not yet been recruited by professional clubs or been unable to join one of the Pôles Espoirs for young hopefuls or the prestigious INF centre at Clairefontaine.

'We have players who come from all over Île-de-France,'

says the new president, Pascal Antonetti. 'Some parents don't think twice about travelling 80 kilometres to bring their children to us.'

This success is the reward for the long-term work undertaken by his predecessors. In 30 years of effort, the club with 900 members has succeeded in developing a real training policy. In the early 1990s, it founded a sports section for the *département* in partnership with the Collège Victor Schoelcher to offer players a full timetable to allow them to train every day without sacrificing their studies. Stéphane Albe, Pogba's new coach, had been in charge since the very beginning. 'Back then they also preferred to pay the instructors top dollar rather than the first team players,' continues Nicolas Damont, who has taken charge of almost every age category at Torcy at one time or another. It has borne fruit: the U13 team regularly qualify for the finals of the National Cup; the U14 and U15 teams play at the highest regional level and, at the U17 and U19 levels in particular, Torcy is the only Seine-et-Marne club to take part in the French championship and to test themselves every weekend against teams from professional clubs. All this makes them very attractive. '2006 was particularly fruitful. We entered into a partnership with Paris Saint-Germain and even finished as the third best club for young players in Île-de-France. That helped us to get more quality young players to come here. But despite competition from a club like Créteil, it was logical that Paul would join us. His membership was officially registered on 3 July 2006,' says Jean-Pierre Damont.

The US Torcy Under-14 team trains three times a week at the Stade du Frémoy. It's a quiet spot, in the middle of a neighbourhood with a village feel. The entrance is welcoming, bordered by a stone wall that overlooks the main pitch. A large athletics track encircles the rectangle of turf.

Behind the stand and the dressing room – named after Guillaume-Ringot in 2008 as a tribute to a player who died after being struck by lightning – is an artificial pitch a little further on that replaced the old dirt pitch in 2010. It faces the water tower and a handful of townhouses with large chimneys on their red roofs. It was here that Paul would come every afternoon on Monday, Tuesday and Thursday. 'The pace of the sessions was quite intense and you had to be careful to protect against injuries, especially to the heel. Dirt pitches are not all that good when you're still growing.'

Stéphane Albe took great care of his new recruit; to make sure Paul, who had just had to repeat Year 8, did not have to change schools and could take part in every session, the two clubs introduced a tailor-made solution: 'It would have been very difficult by public transport because Roissy-en-Brie is not all that well served. So we all had to do our bit: his former instructors at Roissy would bring him here and I would take him back to La Renardière after training and weekend matches. We made the journey with Christopher Mve Bekale,' remembers Albe, his only coach at Torcy. 'They would both get into the back of my khaki Ford Mondeo, which was in a terrible state but it was fine because the kids' boots were always covered in earth!

'I've got some really good memories of those trips. We didn't notice the twenty minutes it took. He would tell me about his mum, whom we didn't see very often because she had to work a lot. They would also take the mickey out of their friends and sometimes I had to get involved. I remember that I would often go back over the matches with Paul in the car, whether they won or not. Like every kid, he had a tendency to put himself down but he also had a good sense of self-criticism and analysed his matches pretty well.'

After the blue and red of Roissy, at age thirteen Paul wore the yellow and red shirt of US Torcy. He would not regret his decision. Alongside Christopher Mve Bekale, he became part of an ultra-competitive squad. This competition did not frighten the new recruit; on the contrary. 'He had no problem integrating into the squad that had played together for several years because he already knew most of the players,' explains Stéphane Albe. Because he got on very well with everyone and had a great relationship with his teammates, it wasn't long before I gave him the captain's armband.'

For his first year in eleven-a-side football, Paul went straight into the midfield. Although at that age there is a tendency to avoid fixing a player in a particular position to allow them to play in different parts of the pitch, he nevertheless found himself there regularly. Usually as a defensive midfielder, but also as a box-to-box midfielder or a number 10: 'It was a treat to see him play,' remembers Jean-Pierre Damont. 'He had some incredible qualities. Getting through a defence was something that was already instinctive to him. Sometimes his instructors had to insist on substituting him because he would take too long to come back and defend.'

'It's true that he liked to go a long way out of his position,' confirms Stéphane Albe. 'He already had his own way of coming forward, of breaking through. He was capable of taking out several players with a sidestep and of making an impressive difference. He would run about all over the place, never trying to save any energy. How many goals did he score like that with us? By picking up the ball before speeding up, getting support from another player and then scoring? It must have been at least a dozen. He didn't need to play in an attacking position to be decisive, he always wanted to score. It was really crazy. If we won, it was fine, but if he didn't score, it was really annoying.'

US Torcy gave a good account of themselves in the Under-14 league. They could compete against the best teams in Île-de-France. The yellow and reds strung together some good performances and finished 'second or third in the table', according to Albe, just behind CS Brétigny. His new captain was very much involved in this fantastic season: 'He brought a lot to the team, through his play, of course, but also through his charisma and mindset. For a thirteen-year-old kid it's never easy to find your feet quickly at a new club. Most would have had a difficult first season, but not him. He was really popular with his teammates and was a delight to coach. He left a good impression as a footballer. I remember him as a kid who was a pleasure to watch. He was always smiling, always happy and nice to everyone. I've been at the club for 23 years and have seen a lot of kids come through. I can honestly say that I've seen very few with his talent and especially his love of the game.'

Paul was also loyal. He had not forgotten his friends at Roissy-en-Brie. He could often be found in the small stand at the Stade Paul-Bessuard supporting his former teammates. Wearing his Torcy tracksuit. 'Of course, we would be mean to him for laughs. But his presence proved that he remained very fond of our club,' remembers Doudou Konte. 'I don't think he had the same connection with Torcy,' says a member of the Roissy club. 'He couldn't go back there on his own because he would know hardly anyone now'. However, if truth be told, he did not really have the time to grow attached.

Chapter 6

Under the Watchful Eye of the Scouts

A few months and then he was gone. In a flash! 'We would have loved to have kept him for longer,' explains the former president, Jean-Pierre Damont. 'Whenever a thirteen- or fourteen-year-old kid leaves for a pre-training course you always wonder. It usually ends up in an internal debate, but if the family really wants them to leave there isn't much we can do but hope it will work out for the player.'

Paul would not spend another season at US Torcy. Unsurprisingly, professional clubs were knocking on his door after his performances in the Under-14 league. Damont goes on to explain: 'We weren't necessarily surprised but a bit disappointed to have found out after the fact.'

In some ways this was the lot of the Seine-et-Marne club, which often served as a springboard for young footballers. At the Stade de Frémoy, they had been used for several years to seeing a parade of scouts and recruiters from professional clubs in France and sometimes abroad pass through every weekend. They were a regular sight in the small stand or behind the railings. 'It's been like that since Mourad Meghni in the early 2000s. When he left Torcy first for AS Cannes and then Bologna it brought our club into the spotlight. Since then, lots of recruiters started prowling around our pitches and some instructors have even tried to grab the young players.'

Nothing like that had happened to Paul but it did not take the professional clubs long to get wind of the 1993 generation playing at US Torcy. The quality of the squad and its convincing results soon spurred the recruitment teams at clubs in Ligue 1 and Ligue 2 into action. 'There were recruiters at all our matches,' remembers Stéphane Albe. It was in this context that observers from Le Havre arrived: 'The first time I saw Paul Pogba was in 2006. What struck me was the accuracy he already had in the long game and I immediately told Oualid about him,' Grégory Agelisas said briefly during an interview with *TF1*.

At this time, Agelisas and Oualid Tanazefti were the two Le Havre Athletic Club scouts for the Paris region. The duo were part of the HAC recruitment team assembled by Franck Sale: 'They were two engaging young people who I was lucky enough to train. It gave me a chance to launch them and teach them about the profession. They had a "good eye", were familiar with the clubs in the Paris region and had brought quite a lot of players to Le Havre, including that same year Benjamin Mendy (now of Manchester City), whom they had found at the Palaiseau club.'

Tanazefti would take his turn to see the 'little gem' play, as well as the other players he had heard about. This former goalkeeper, who had played for CA Lisieux and Pacy, had been forced to give up football at the age of eighteen due to an ankle injury. He was not much older when he went to the Val d'Oise *département* to attend an Under-14 league match between the local club of Entente Sannois-Saint Gratien and US Torcy. He understood immediately that he had a champion in his midst. Franck Sale was kept updated by his two observers: 'They told me they had seen some great players, particularly a phenomenon called Paul Pogba. So I made the trip down. The first time I saw him play it wasn't with

Torcy but in his home neighbourhood of La Renardière, at the City Stade, with his friends. That might seem surprising but it was something that was quite common at the time. It allowed us to see players in a different context and it was often very revealing. I discovered a very confident lad that day, he was a leader and very charismatic. An athlete too. You don't see players with that kind of potential every day when you work as a recruiter. We needed to be quick off the mark and not lose any time because there wasn't much competition at that stage.'

Strangely, Paris Saint-Germain, US Torcy's partner at the forefront of football in the Île-de-France region, did not seem to have spotted the player. Unlike Olympique Lyonnais and AJ Auxerre. The heads of recruitment at the two clubs confirmed: 'We had been following him for some time. He had been flagged up thanks to his profile as one of the players we had already heard plenty of talk about,' said Gérard Bonneau, from Lyon. His counterpart in Auxerre, Vincent Cabin, confirmed: 'We had also heard his name. We had gone to Roissy-en-Brie to see him with the former director of the training academy, Daniel Rolland. But Le Havre got there first.'

The Normandy club were soon in contact with Paul's family, via Oualid Tanazefti, who had got hold of the phone number of his mother, Yeo Moriba, and convinced her to allow her son to visit HAC for a trial. Paul was invited to attend in early November 2006. About thirty players, including several 'Parisians' were brought together for a few days to take a series of tests at the Le Havre academy. They were summoned to number 32, Rue de la Cavée Verte at the Stade Argentin. Behind the railings, under the trees surrounding the complex, all the members of the academy staff came together on the three pitches to assess the potential recruits; as well as the academy director, Jean-Marc Nobilo, the pre-training and academy coaches were also in attendance. These included Mickaël Le Baillif, the Under-14 instructor: 'There were a few boys with different qualities; Paul demonstrated plenty of technical talent. He was tall and skinny and despite his height, he showed great technical skill. The decision whether to take him or not was a group one as always.'

The members of the recruitment team were present, as they are at every trial. Franck Sale was there, as was Oualid Tanazefti, who had made the journey to Normandy. Tanazefti believed his presence was crucial to the recruitment of Paul: 'His trial was fantastic but there were only two or three of us who thought so,' he told *Le Pays d'Auge* in 2016. 'The coaches thought it had been a good trial but they weren't keen on Paul Pogba. I had to cheat a bit to get him into the last group. I insisted that he play. After that Franck Sale and I managed to get him to sign because Auxerre and Lyon were both waiting in the wings.'

Torcy were left out of the negotiations. 'It wasn't that we wanted to go behind their back,' confirms Franck Sale, 'but when we see a boy with a lot of potential, we work discreetly to avoid attracting lots of attention.' The deal was therefore done with a minimum of fuss in November 2006.

The head of recruitment had taken the trouble to explain the plan for the youngster at length to his parents.

'There was, of course, his schooling, which was paramount to us, as well as his long-term career in the sport. His parents were very excited.' So much so that they asked Le Havre to take his two older brothers, Florentin and Mathias, now aged sixteen, into the academy as well. The twins also had a trial but the competition was too tough for their generation.

There was a party atmosphere at Paul's father's apartment in Roissy-en-Brie. By late autumn Paul Pogba's future was sealed. Franck Sale and Oualid Tanazefti were there to provide Paul's official welcome to Le Havre and they had not come empty-handed. A small cardboard folder contained the famous contract: a non-solicitation agreement. These allow professional clubs with training academies to bind themselves to players aged under thirteen on 31 December of the year of signature. These contracts also protect the club from approaches from other French clubs for three years and guarantee the player the chance to sign an apprentice contract over the two subsequent seasons.

'It really was a great night,' remembers Franck Sale. 'We talked about football because his father was also very smart and passionate. He had strong convictions when it came to educating his children. We talked for hours about Guinea and African football, almost forgetting why we had come. It was 3 o'clock in the morning by the time we noticed the contract still had to be signed. We had to wake Paul up so he could sign it. It was a bit surreal.'

US Torcy did not find out that the Pogba family had signed an agreement with the Le Havre Athletic Club until after that night. How did they take the news, which came barely halfway through the season? 'Let's just say that it wasn't very harmonious and things were not all that calm when he left,' says Jean-Pierre Damont, with regret. Stéphane Albe is more tempered: 'It wasn't a problem for us that Paul had a trial and signed for Le Havre, even if our goal was to get players to stay for as long as possible. The question was whether he had left too soon. Obviously there is no hard and fast rule, but we had seen so many failures. I can only remember two successes after such early departures: Paul, of course, and a central defender, Christopher Jullien, who signed for

AJ Auxerre at age twelve [after moving to SC Freiburg, he has been at Toulouse since 2016]. Whatever the case, it's up to the family and the player; the club can't get involved.'

For the Pogba family it was a leap. Yeo Moriba was about to let her youngest son fly away from the family apartment to somewhere just over 200 kilometres away. One can only imagine the stress and heartache for his mother, knowing that her twins were also about to leave not just the Paris region, but France as well. Florentin and Mathias had been recruited by the Spanish club Celta Vigo, where they were about to join its academy. She was even prepared to sacrifice her own happiness to allow her sons to live out their passion.

Chapter 7

In Safe Harbour

The wind sweeps over the docks, bringing spray and a characteristic salty tang with it. Colours blend together under a changing sky: from green to blue to red, a rainbow of containers ready to go to sea. The occasional silence is broken by a chorus of dull thuds. The gigantic sky blue structures, as tall as cathedrals, perform a ballet whenever they are required to load or unload the cargo ships. The berths have names that are so familiar to those who spend almost every waking hour here: René Coty, de l'Eure, Marcel Despujois, Vétillard, Théophile Ducrocq and Vauban, where ships of all sizes come to rest after arriving along the Grand Canal or the Canal de Tancarville. This is Le Havre. More precisely, the port of Le Havre, the second largest in France after that of Marseille.

This impressive facility goes back a long way. It has been there for 500 years, looking out onto the English Channel, built originally on the orders of King Francis I. It has seen plenty of history: in the seventeenth century, it was the departure point for long-distance expeditions to the Americas to trade in tobacco, coffee, spices, cotton and sugar. At the same time, slave ships were setting a course for Africa to pick up their human cargo. Ferries kept alive the link with Portsmouth in England for a long time, but they now make the trip less frequently. Nowadays the harbour is busy with single-handed yacht races, family reunions on pleasure craft and fishing boats unloading scallops and langoustines onto the quays at Saint-Thomas.

It is the gateway to the city to which it gave birth. A city on two levels linked by a funicular. The lower city, ravaged by the Second World War and rebuilt in concrete by Auguste Perret, where the huge Saint-Joseph Church serves as a landmark in the local sky and the 'Volcan' – a spurt of white magma that rose up from the earth in 1982 to house a cultural centre – looks like a UFO in a city centre that had to be completely redesigned. The upper part of Le Havre was fortunately spared from British bombing. Peaceful, it overlooks the port, with the city's working-class districts to the east next to more upmarket residential homes.

But it is further down, close to the expanses of shingle and colourful beach huts with rounded roofs that the heart of the city beats. The docks are home to numerous cultural and artistic projects that help bring the place out of its post-industrial torpor. They act as a reminder that before it sank into crisis and gloominess, Le Havre had often been quicker off the mark than its rival Rouen, particularly on the sporting front. The Saint Thomas basketball club was the first to register with the French federation in 1932. Despite never having won a national title, it has long been part of the elite and launched the careers of several players, such as the American wing for the Spurs, Bruce Bowen.

And what of the Le Havre Athletic Club (HAC), often referred to as the doyen of French and European football? Unsurprisingly, it was British workers at the port who were responsible for its foundation in 1872, first as the Le Havre Football Club, then as the Le Havre Athletic Club, when it became a multi-sports club twelve years later. It is now an important player. 'It's an institution,' says the journalist, Benoît Donkele in the offices of *Paris-Normandie* on

Boulevard de Strasbourg. 'The club experienced some fantastic years during the 1950s, when it won the Coupe de France [1959]. Since then not much has happened and HAC now has the image of a training club that has been a springboard for a number of international players.'

The list of professionals who have passed through the club's academy or been thrown in at the deep end at the La Cavée Verte, Jules-Deschaseaux and Océane stadiums, since July 2012, is as long as Boulevard Clémenceau: Michel Hidalgo, Ibrahim Ba, Jean-Alain Boumsong and Vikash Dhorasoo, to name but a few. Since the early 2000s, it has seen plenty of shooting stars: Anthony Le Tallec (Liverpool and Sunderland), Florent Sinama Pongolle (Liverpool and Atlético Madrid) and Charles N'Zogbia (Newcastle, Wigan and Aston Villa); experienced Bleus, Dimitri Payet (West Ham and Olympique Marseille), Steve Mandanda (OM and Crystal Palace) and Lassana Diarra (Chelsea, Arsenal, Portsmouth, Real Madrid and OM); as well as a handful of hidden gems playing in the Premier League, Riyad Mahrez (Leicester City), in the Bundesliga, Pierre-Emerick Aubameyang (Borussia Dortmund) and even in France, Benjamin Mendy (Manchester City). Not to mention Paul Pogba, who arrived in the city in the summer of 2007.

The Cavée Verte academy is located in the upper part of the city, in a residential neighbourhood where buildings rarely exceed two or three storeys. It is a place full of history because, after having played its first matches on a vacant lot in Avenue Foch, HAC took advantage of the arrival of the Swiss Albert Shadegg to move two kilometres away to Rue de la Cavée Verte in 1915. The Hacmen, as they are known, played here for more than half a century. After the construction of the Stade Jules-Deschaseaux in 1971, it became the reserve team pitch then base camp for the Le Havre academy from 1980.

It is unlikely that Paul Pogba was aware of this history when he arrived in Le Havre in July 2007. Like many successful candidates from the Paris region, he set his course towards Seine-Maritime just as he was enjoying his final year of pre-training, in the Under-15 age category. The port city is a little over 200 kilometres from the family home and two and a half hours by car along the A13 *autoroute*. 'Parisians often join us at that age to strengthen our squads made up primarily of players from the region,' explains the former academy director, Alain Olio, who has been in charge of the Académie du Dakar Sacré Cœur in Senegal for two years now.

The building does not look like much, with large windows reminiscent of old-fashioned constructions of the 1980s and 90s. Trophies won by the youth teams of the light blue and dark blue club are on display at the entrance. A little further on, the oldest part of the building is home to a large spiral staircase that goes up to three pitches, two of which are artificial. The dressing rooms and weights room are on the ground floor, close to the main entrance, where the club proudly displays the photos of some of the big names who have passed through its doors. There are about 30 of them. On this wall of legends, Paul Pogba appears next to the goal-keeper Steve Mandanda, in action during a match with the France team. 'He didn't stay long enough for us to have photos of him in the club shirt,' says an employee, almost apologetically.

The bedrooms are upstairs, with two distinct areas separated by a common room: one is for academy residents aged from sixteen to nineteen and the other for seven or eight players from pre-training, aged thirteen and fourteen. It was here that the former midfielder from Roissy-en-Brie and Torcy laid his hat in a room he would soon share, according to his coaches, with his great friend El-Hadji Ba (Sunderland and Charlton), recruited the same year from CSL Aulnay-sous-Bois.

A new life was beginning and adapting is never easy. 'It takes five to six months because the rhythm is intense,' says Bunel. 'Paul would finish school every day at 3.30pm and he had about 30 minutes to get to the academy by minibus, drop off his school stuff, change and be on the pitch by 4pm. Training would last for two hours, usually at the Cavée Verte but sometimes at the Stade Auguste-Delaune when the weather was bad. He would then have to do his homework and tutoring. Dinner was served at 7pm, followed by free time with his instructors.' Weekends were devoted to competition, with matches on Sunday, but the 'Parisians' had the right to special treatment: 'For us it was really important that they got to see their families,' confirms Alain Olio. 'We set up a routine so they could go home one weekend out of every three.'

On the pitch, Paul found himself part of a talented 1993 generation that included about twenty players, including some future professionals: among the hot shots were his roommate El-Hadji Ba, as well as the defender Prince-Désir Gouano (Centre de Formation de Paris), who would later end up at Juventus before playing in the Dutch (RKC Waalwijk), English (Bolton) and Turkish (Gaziantepspor) leagues. There were also two players from the 1994 generation who often played above their age category: a former defender from US Palaiseau, Benjamin Mendy, and a talented goalkeeper, Brice Samba, who had arrived a year earlier from ALM Évreux.

Mickaël Le Baillif was their coach, Paul Pogba's first at Le Havre: 'Paul came from an amateur club, and without knocking them, there were things that needed to be put in place,' says the former coach, who has remained loyal to HAC. 'He was still playing a very pure and natural form of football. He had a tendency not to follow instructions. During his first season, we also had to teach him how to get more of a handle on his emotions.'

During the 2007–08 season, Le Havre took a leading role in the Under-15 league. Despite fierce competition from the professional stables of Paris Saint-Germain, Stade Malherbe from Caen and Amiens SC, as well as the presence in the group of numerous well respected amateur clubs, Le Havre held their own. 'We had a very good season,' remembers Mickaël Le Baillif. In a system with two defensive midfielders, 'Paul grew in strength over the course of the games. We finished second in the league behind PSG, but in both matches Paul played a prominent role and had been one of the best on the pitch.'

He confirmed his ability to get the best out of himself in important matches during the Coupe National that saw regional teams face off against each other on the pitches of the national centre at Clairefontaine at the end of the season. Every year, this competition brings together the elite of the age category and usually offers the chance to spot the fifty or so players who will go on to make up the Under-16 France team the following season. 'Paul Pogba was the captain of the Normandy team that included seven or eight players from the Le Havre club,' explains a member of the French Federation. He clearly stood out from the crowd. His presence and work rate were immediately obvious, even if he lost a lot of balls. He was the only one we were talking about.' Vincent Cabin, AJ Auxerre's representative at the competition, confirms: 'It was the first time I'd seen him again since he'd signed for Le Havre and he really did get himself noticed.'

The Normandy team played their part but eventually lost out to stronger opposition. It was the team from Île-de-France who won the 33rd Coupe Nationale. As always, Paul struggled to hide his disappointment. Despite the tears and anger, he came to realise the progress he had made in just one season. What was not clear, however, was whether he was aware of the extent of the possibilities that were opening up to him.

Chapter 8

Devils in the Flesh

---

28 October 2008. Stade Auguste-Delaune in Maison-Alfort, to the south-east of Paris. The France Under-16 team were preparing to play their first game in the Val-de-Marne tournament that offered a tempting draw in its tenth year, with Italy, the Netherlands and Uruguay in attendance. The competition is a classic, the first test for the generation given the honour of being selected to take part. That year, the majority of the players had been spotted by Guy Ferrier at the Under-15 Coupe Nationale at Clairefontaine. After a battery of tests at the end of the summer, the very best players were given the opportunity to make their debut in a blue shirt during two friendlies played in Wales that September. But this was their first official call-up, the first title waiting to be won in a Tricolore shirt.

A few minutes before kick-off, Paul Pogba was getting ready in the small dressing room next to the pitch. Staring off into the distance, he was sitting next to the door at the end of the wooden bench that ran around the room. He listened to the final words of advice from his manager, pulled on his number 6 red shirt and white shorts, adjusted the captain's armband on his left arm and took one last sip of water before standing up. The time had come for the duel against Uruguay.

Crowds in the stand were sparse that Tuesday afternoon. The atmosphere was far from electric but there were still plenty of kids, parents, ardent football fans, and, as always at these international matches, plenty of scouts from France and abroad who had come to see what the 1993 generation could do for the first time.

Winning his third cap, Paul found himself in the midfield alongside the Strasbourg player, Marco Rosenfelder. The duo were charged with resisting the onslaught of the *Celeste* and supplying the two strikers. The plan worked well, as the defence held firm and Yaya Sanogo found two openings up front at the beginning of the second half.

'Satisfactory but could do much better.' This was the assessment of the first match provided by the manager, Guy Ferrier, who retired to Lot-et-Garonne in November 2015 after more than 60 years in football. 'He certainly worked hard, but he always went too far. He thought he could manage everything himself. To get him to make progress, all I had to do was point out to him what he was doing wrong.'

This analysis was similar to that of the coaches at Le Havre who had taken over from Mickaël Le Baillif when *La Pioche* joined the academy. 'The first months of the 2008–09 season weren't easy for him,' explains François Rodrigues, who spent ten years in Normandy before joining the PSG academy in 2010. 'Even with his international status, he had trouble focusing. Instead of playing above his age category with me in the Under-17 national team, he played for the Under-16s with Michaël Bunel, where he would sometimes score four or five goals in one game. I wanted to leave him some time to think about it but it didn't really work because he loved football so much that for him just playing was enough whatever the level.'

In the stands at the Stade Auguste-Delaune in Maison-Alfort was someone who did not necessarily share this opinion. As soon as the final whistle had blown, he picked up his phone to talk to his superiors: 'I called Geoff Watson, head scout at the academy to tell him I'd just seen a player we should be very interested in. He told me to keep following him closely and to do my job. The director of the academy, Jimmy Ryan, joined me for the next game to see the player for himself.'

This anecdote comes from David Friio, now a scout at AS Saint-Étienne. It left its mark on his career. Born in Thionville in Moselle in 1973, this tall, dark-haired man with a carefully trimmed beard spent a long time as a midfielder in the French second division with Épinal and Nîmes before deciding to cross the Channel in the early 2000s to Plymouth Argyle, ending his career with Nottingham Forest in the Championship five years later. This experience gave him the opportunity to win second and third division titles with Plymouth Argyle in 2002 and 2004 respectively, learn English and build a decent network of contacts. It was this background that helped him become Manchester United's recruiter in France in early 2009. 'I had been working for the Red Devils for just six months and when I saw Paul that day I said to myself that he had the profile to play at United. Of course, with his lanky physique it was clear that he didn't find running easy because he was still growing. But he had exceptional touch. He gave himself time on the ball and shone because of that. From that game onwards I began following him with the France team and his club to see if my first impression had been right.'

The United recruiter was a particularly attentive spectator during the Bleus' last two matches in the Val-de-Marne tournament. During the 1–0 win over the Netherlands and the convincing 4–0 victory over Italy, David Friio scrutinised the French number 6 in minute detail: 'You noticed him first as a player because of his physique, technical skill and vision, but then we had to dig a little deeper. With Paul it was confirmation after confirmation! He ticked every box. He was also a leader on the pitch and he loved to really fire the ball with his long legs.'

Whether it was with the Bleus or for his club, Paul was making great progress. On the pitches of the Cavée Verte, he put in plenty of effort at the daily training sessions. Oualid Tanazefti, who had spotted him at Torcy, was among his first supporters and often there to keep his morale up. His coaches did not go easy on him. 'We often had long discussions. We tried to explain his choices to him, to give him tips,' remembers Michaël Bunel. His counterpart, François Rodrigues, was always ready to offer extra advice to the young midfielder. At the end of almost every session, when the rest of the team were already in the showers, Paul stayed behind on the pitch to work on his long game and learn to use every part of his foot. 'Great cross, Paulo,' the Under-17 national team coach praised. 'Not a floating ball but a firm ball, that's it.' Paul listened quietly and would not forget to thank his instructor when the time came.

David Friio was casting a watchful eye from the wings. In early September, he went to the south-west of France to attend two friendlies against Portugal. In January, he made several return trips to Le Havre to watch his 'protégé' at work in the light and dark blue strip. It was one revelation after another. Paul had reached another milestone and carried his team to within touching distance in the fight with Racing Club de Lens for first place in Group A of the Under-17 national championship. Friio approached his representatives: 'I organised a meeting with Gaël Mahé, who had a mandate to represent him until he turned eighteen, and with Bruno Satin, an agent who often worked with Manchester United. We talked about the Red Devils' interest in Paul and

Mahé was excited. All that remained was to meet the family and offer them a trip to Manchester to visit the club facilities and meet Sir Alex Ferguson.'

How would they react in the apartment in Roissy-en-Brie when they heard the news? With screams, excitement and sparkling eyes: the words 'Manchester' and 'Ferguson' sounded like a dream to the Pogba family. The year got off to a good start when their son scored his first goal for the Bleus in Manisa in Turkey during the 2–1 win over Norway in the Aegean Cup.

The meeting in Manchester was set for mid-March. It was a wonderful way to celebrate the young international's sixteenth birthday. Antoine Pogba, Yeo Moriba, Gaël Mahé and David Friio went with Paul on this trip to the theatre of dreams. 'We arrived in England the day before so we had a full day there,' explains the former Manchester United recruiter. 'That morning at breakfast I gave Paul's dad my red club tie. He was so proud to wear it on that special day. We took a detour through the city centre then went to the academy and bumped into the first team. Cristiano Ronaldo was still at Man U back then and he said hello to everyone. We took a tour of the facilities, visited the stadium and then went to Sir Alex Ferguson's office. It lasted almost an hour. The club manager took the time to explain the Red Devils' philosophy to the family. They hung on Ferguson's every word. I acted as the interpreter. He told them that age wasn't a barrier here, that they had no problem promoting young talented players. He hit the nail on the head. He really knew how to do that! I can tell you that by the time we left the office to go back to France, the kid had already made up his mind. He knew that that was where he wanted to play, at least that was the impression I had.'

Back in Le Havre, Paul did not seem unduly perturbed

to have been courted by the king of Manchester United. It did not affect his performance in any case. He continued to imprcss in every match at the end of the 2008–09 season. Whether it was with the France team at the Montaigu tournament in the Vendée, where scouts from Spanish and English clubs made nothing but positive notes about the France midfielder in their notebooks, or at club level, where the boy from Lagny-sur-Marne delighted his teammates. Thanks to a superb second half of the season, François Rodrigues's team claimed one of eight spots for the final Under-17 phase. Finishing second in their group, the boys from HAC found themselves in Moulins, in the Allier, in late May alongside Lens, Nancy and Lyon to compete in a mini-league, the winner of which would claim a place in the final of the French championship: 'He played well against Lyon and was brilliant in our second game against Nancy,' remembers his coach. 'When we were losing 1–0 and a man down, he swept away everything in his path. He scored the equaliser then the winner with an exceptional goal: he picked up the ball in midfield, got past two players then unleashed an incredible strike that left the goalkeeper with no chance at all. We eventually missed out on qualification, losing 2–1 to Lens in the final game. Despite the fact that we were knocked out, Paul had done very well and was one of the best players on the pitch.'

It was with this defeat that Paul Pogba's second season in Le Havre came to an end. Although they had not been told, his coaches and teammates sensed that something was going on behind the scenes. 'There were plenty of rumours towards the end of the season and there were always lots of people hanging around him,' remembers François Rodrigues. 'But at our level there wasn't much we could do other than trust the management of the club. So we went off on holiday and when we came back we found out he'd decided to leave.'

Chapter 9

Stolen

Paul Pogba signed for Manchester United on 30 July 2009. Le Havre saw their golden nugget slip through their fingers. It was initially very hard to understand given that the Lagny-sur-Marne native had signed a non-solicitation agreement on arrival that was supposed to lead to an apprentice contract. When the news came out, those in charge at the Le Havre club made their anger and dismay clear in a statement that expressed their indignation regarding the dealings of Manchester United's directors' who had not respected the contract and offered 'very high sums of money to the parents of the [player] with the aim of obtaining the transfer of their son to England.'

Published on 31 July, the Normandy club was using this text to assert its desire not to be pushed around. The club was unfortunately accustomed to these practices: in 2001, the pair of Florent Sinama Pongolle and Anthony Le Tallec had been tempted by Liverpool, then, in 2006, HAC had to handle the unexpected departure of Matthias Lepiller for Fiorentina. But it was the Charles N'Zogbia affair that had caused the biggest commotion. At that time, the promising eighteen-year-old midfielder was recruited by Newcastle United while he was under a training contract. After three years of proceedings, the Court of Arbitration for Sport eventually delivered its verdict, holding that 'Charles N'Zogbia and Newcastle United were in breach of contractual obligations.' The Le Havre club was awarded €900,000 in compensation.

Le Havre was not the only French training club to find itself under threat from European 'predators': in 2000, the departure of Mourad Meghni from AS Cannes for Bologna had provoked indignation. The practice of poaching young players had not stopped, as demonstrated by the case of Gaël Kakuta, a midfielder born in 1991 who chose to break his contract with Racing Club de Lens to join Chelsea in 2009: the London club was initially sanctioned by FIFA to pay the sum of €910,000 and, most importantly, was banned from recruiting for two years. But, in order to avoid this unfortunate punishment that risked weakening the club's ambitions in Europe, Chelsea eventually put their hands in their pockets and reached a financial agreement with Lens that was later ratified by the Court of Arbitration for Sport.

In Manchester there was no doubt that the case of Pogba had nothing to do with the N'Zogbia and Kakuta affairs: 'Quite simply because the non-solicitation agreement signed by Paul with Le Havre was only valid between French clubs. It was only a non-aggression pact with other teams in France. Nothing more,' explains Yves Martin, the sports adviser who worked with Gaël Mahé from 2004 to 2013. Moreover, 'if the directors at Le Havre had really wanted to protect him, they could have had him sign an elite contract and then there would have been nothing more to say. But they didn't do that, although the player was captain of the France team and therefore subject to plenty of attention. How can you complain of theft when you leave the car with its doors wide open and the keys in the ignition?'

It is a vivid image but one that demonstrates the fantastic opportunity open to foreign clubs when it comes to shopping in France's training academies: 'When it comes down to it, French legislation penalises its own clubs more than their foreign counterparts,' says the agent Bruno Satin, one of the intermediaries in this deal, also involved, among others, in the departure of Gerard Piqué from Barcelona to Manchester United in 2004.

France was not the only shopping destination for the English club. At the same time, the Red Devils were on the point of signing the young central defender from Fiorentina, Michele Fornasier.

Why, then, aware of the potential problems, did Le Havre not protect themselves better? 'They didn't believe in Paul Pogba, it's as simple as that,' claim insiders who were close to the player. 'He couldn't be made to sign an apprentice contract yet, quite simply because he was a year behind at school and French law required him to be in Year 11 before he could sign such a contract,' an HAC instructor countered.

One possible explanation can be found in the upheaval that took place at the HAC academy during the 2008–09 season. A change in the director of an academy is never without consequences. That year, Alain Olio was replaced by Frédéric Lipka, the former general manager of Racing Club de France. The former French third division player arrived at the Cavée Verte with plenty of ambition. At 39 years of age, this appointment was a real chance for him to progress at a club recognised for its training. But Lipka soon found himself having to deal with the Pogba affair: 'I arrived in August and Paul immediately began getting call-ups for the France team. The case needed to be handled urgently, but at that point I wasn't familiar yet with all the ins and outs,' he remembers, from New York, where he now works for the MLS (Major League Soccer). 'I did everything within my power to try to keep the kid. Franck Sale, the head of recruitment and I had meeting after meeting with the legal boards.

Franck met his family. I asked Paul to come to my office and I still remember a kid who didn't really want to leave. He was happy with us, with his friends. But his advisers pushed him to leave and of course when it's a Ligue 2 club against Manchester United, it's hard to put up a fight. It's a bit like David and Goliath.'

The president of the Le Havre Athletic Club was also trying to reverse the trend. Jean-Pierre Louvel was an influential man in French football. He had been in charge of his club for almost eight years and had just been named head of the French Union of Professional Football Clubs. He had plenty of experience of this kind of thing having already overseen the Lepiller and N'Zogbia affairs. 'We were criticised for not having locked down the file by offering Paul an apprentice contract at the end of the 2007–08 season but it wasn't that simple,' explains the man who remained loyal to the club until 2015. 'This type of case can be a real dilemma for clubs and their trainers. Obviously, to protect themselves they need to get all players under contract as quickly as possible, but they have to deserve it. Paul had undeniable qualities, but his coaches wanted to stimulate him and not bring him on too quickly. In 2008, the director of our academy was opposed to having him sign an apprentice pre-contract. And I understood his decision, which had only been taken for the good of the player. I also understood the reaction of his parents' representatives, who may well have been irritated by this. Of course, it weakened our position because, from the moment we found out other clubs were interested in him, we tried to put things right but by then it was already too late.'

The door had been left ajar to potential suitors and it would remain that way. The Le Havre player's performances for the France team had alerted several major European clubs tempted by the opportunity to pick up this great hope for small change, aware that training compensation generally amounted to around €150,000. 'Every recruiter and talent scout found out about Pogba during the 2008–09 season,' claims the sports adviser Yves Martin, in a singsong accent that betrays his origins in the South of France. 'Plenty of teams were after him. Manchester United, of course, and two other English clubs, Chelsea and Arsenal.' 'That's true,' confirms David Friio. 'But not Manchester City, as some have said. The Citizens did not yet have a policy of recruiting young players. On the other hand, Spanish clubs were also interested, but our main competitor was French.'

It was none other than Olympique Lyonnais, who had just won a series of seven consecutive French league titles between 2002 and 2008. As surprising as it may seem, it was Le Havre that played the role of intermediary: 'There was indeed a discussion with Lyon at one point,' confirms Jean-Pierre Louvel. 'If he was going to leave, it was better that it should benefit a French club.' Paul Pogba was welcomed in Lyon at the Tola-Vologe Academy by its director, Rémi Garde, and head of recruitment, Gérard Bonneau. 'We had the opportunity for a visit from the player's parents,' remembers the latter. 'His mother seemed very excited about our plan, but it didn't take long before we realised that it would be tough to seal the deal. His advisers wanted him to go to England at all costs and they wanted money.'

According to leaks in the French media, Manchester United were reported to have offered '€100,000 to both his parents and a house so his mother could come to live with him in Manchester.'

'Not true,' according to David Friio. 'Pogba's parents never sold their child to our club, that's nonsense. For us, it's never a question of money in these age categories, it's a question of play. He was subject to the charter, like all young players at the academy, with a salary cap until he turned seventeen, nothing more.' The sports adviser Yves Martin is more measured: 'There was a proper three-year plan for his football that allowed him to join the academy, train with the reserve team and occasionally with the professionals. But there were also a few things in return: the club found them an apartment and provided them with a driver. His mother also had to sign an employment contract and earn an income for looking after her son. It was around that time that we went to fetch his two brothers from Spain.' They were being exploited at Celta Vigo, where they were playing for €200 a month with accommodation and food. We placed Florentin at Sedan in Ligue 2 and Mathias at Quimper in the fourth division.'

As the twins were preparing to return home, the future of the youngest member of the family would now play out on the other side of the Channel. The decision was confirmed in mid-May 2009, just before the final stages of the French Under-17 league. Unsurprisingly, the Pogba family came to an agreement with Manchester United, after being won over by Sir Alex Ferguson's speech. The time had come to break up with Le Havre. As they had done in 2004 for N'Zogbia, the HAC directors decided to initiate proceedings with FIFA. They were supported by their federation, who upheld their request, blocked the player's release and even ruled him out of selection for almost six months.

This pressure on the part of the French authorities was in vain as on 7 October 2009, Manchester United emerged victorious from the wrangle with the Normandy club: 'Manchester United is pleased to confirm that the Football Association has been authorised by FIFA to register Paul Pogba as a Manchester United player with immediate effect,' the Red Devils proudly announced on their website.

An epilogue to the affair would come in June 2010. After tearing strips off each other, the two clubs eventually found common ground. According to Jean-Pierre Louvel, it was the English club that made contact with him: 'I went to Manchester with our lawyer and we eventually came to a financial agreement. It didn't solve the initial problem, knowing that they had taken a young player from us, but the fact that they agreed to pay a lot more than the €150,000 in training rights showed that they felt they had been in the wrong.'

Chapter 10

Manchester, the Home of Football

'It's not easy to talk to someone about football. Everyone has their own experience, their own knowledge, their own life, their own ideas, their own loves. These are some of the things we think are important when it comes to illustrating the history of the beautiful game, its globalisation and how it's now the most popular sport in the world.' Adam Comstive is interrupted by a petulant child on a school trip who wants to know if you have to pay to play on the table football. The ground floor of the National Football Museum in Manchester is seething with people. A boy wearing white gloves is taking selfies with the FA Cup and Premier League trophies. A curious couple are examining the wall dedicated to champions such as George Best, Jack Charlton and Brenda Sempare.

The schoolboy's urgent question has been answered; Comstive, the museum's senior marketing and digital officer, can continue his tour. 'As I was saying, everyone can find something here that is part of his or her life, like the stickers they collected as a child or the shirt belonging to Diego Armando Maradona, which reminds them of the England Argentina quarter-final and the Hand of God. When they leave here visitors take a story home with them, an image, a memory or they wonder what a statue of Michael Jackson is doing in a football museum.' The museum employee with something of a mad professor about him is not wrong. The three floors of this tall glass and steel building pointing towards the heart of the city offer an infinite number of stories and curiosities. For example, *The Game*, a facsimile copy of the notebook in which Ebenezer Cobb, the secretary of the Football Association, first wrote down the rules of the game in 1863. A little further on a phrase spoken by Arsène Wenger appears highlighted in white: 'The first time I came to England I said to myself, without a doubt, football was created here!' Or a panel that remembers how in 1921 'the FA banned women's teams from its grounds claiming "the game of football is quite unsuitable for females and should not be encouraged". The ban was only lifted in 1971.' There is also the crown that a fan gave to Colin Bell, the Manchester City midfielder, and the painting by Michael Browne of Éric Cantona in the guise of Piero della Francesca's *Risen Christ.* Not to mention George Best's golden ball or the menu from the Majestic Hotel in Belgrade dated 5 February 1958. It is signed by the United players. The following day, eight of them lost their lives in the Munich air disaster. Despite being a national museum there are plenty of relics of the city's two teams. Paul Pogba already knew plenty about United: Ferguson, Scholes, Beckham, Giggs and Cristiano Ronaldo were names he could recite by heart. Despite having sold the Portuguese player to Real Madrid for £80 million and losing against Lionel Messi's Barcelona in the Champions League, the Red Devils were dominating English football. On 16 May 2009, they had won the Premier League for a third consecutive time. In short, for a sixteen-year-old boy joining the United Academy was 'an incredible and unique opportunity that was impossible to refuse,' confirms Michele Fornasier, now

24 and a defender at Pescara, who had arrived at United from Fiorentina a few weeks before Pogba. 'You might hesitate a bit, think about it,' Fornasier goes on, 'because making the leap from Italy or France is a big one, but when it comes down to it you say yes.'

Now, when asked by *Esquire*: 'Was it lonely leaving France for Manchester aged sixteen?' Paul answers without hesitation: 'No, it was beautiful. I learned English, new culture, new country, new friends [sic].' Rose-tinted spectacles are a wonderful thing when looking back. It is true that Oualid Tanzefti, his representative, moved to the city; it's true that Yeo, his mother, joined him, but integrating into a different world, a more physical kind of football and a place where everyone speaks another language, came at a price. 'Good morning, good afternoon, one, two, three, four': Paul Pogba's English vocabulary was limited to a handful of basic words. He found it almost impossible to understand what his teammates were saying with their strange Mancunian accents. 'His English wasn't the best at first, but he was just a chatty, confident guy, and obviously he was confident in his football too. He believed in his ability and he believed in himself,' John Cofie, now a striker with Southport in the National League, would tell *Sky Sports* years later. 'Paul was a joker, lively, friendly. Even if we were nervous before an important match, he would joke around, sing and dance. He was a great player, as he is now. You could see that he was head and shoulders above the others,' remembers Fornasier. 'I played against him for the Republic of Ireland Under-17s against France in the summer before he signed for us,' explains Sean McGinty, now a defender at Torquay United. 'You could tell he was a bit special. He was a big lad, not as big as he is now, he's really put some muscle on, but you could tell in that game that there was something about him. He was fantastic. When Man United announced they'd signed him I thought, wow, this could be a special year for the academy.'

Paul McGuinness is on holiday in the Algarve but he is happy to be interviewed over the phone about the boy he coached for two seasons (2009–10 and 2010–11). McGuinness, the son of Wilf, a former United player and manager, has seen plenty of players pass through the academy in his 23 years, but not all of them have left the impression Paul did when he arrived in Manchester with a glowing report from the scouts. 'The first time I saw him, all six foot three of him, I thought, "Wow, he looks the part." He had a great smile and long levers. Normally at that age, boys are growing and they lack coordination, but he had it. And that was not all … I soon saw he had quick footwork, great ball skills, timing, the ability to drop his shoulder and a lot of confidence. Above all he showed great personality and that he was extremely serious. He was the last to leave the gym and the pitch. He gave 100 per cent and would often stay behind to practise free-kicks and penalties. If someone stole the ball off him at training he would give his all to get it back because he wanted to prove he was someone.'

Pogba played his first match with McGuinness's Young Reds just a few days after FIFA ruled in favour of the English club. On 10 October 2009, the United Academy played Crewe Alexandra at the Gresty Road ground. It ended 2–1 to the Railwaymen. 'Of some consolation was the eye-catching debut from sixteen-year-old French starlet Paul Pogba in midfield,' wrote Ben Hibbs on the United website. 'Pogba spraying passes around from midfield and firing just wide from long-range … continued to impress in the centre of the park. He is very strong on the ball and cultured in possession. Comparisons with Patrick Vieira are inevitable …

Pogba rattled the crossbar with a thunderous free kick with twenty minutes remaining.'

It was a fantastic debut for the boy wearing the number 8. 'His teammates were really impressed: not only was he a big guy and a great footballer but he had an amazing desire to do well and win,' remembers McGuinness, who adds: 'Paul had a really nice attitude and everybody liked him.' Thanks to his character, Paul quickly integrated into the group. There were plenty of good players such as Ravel Morrison, Jesse Lingard, Michael and Will Keane, Tom Thorpe and Ryan Tunnicliffe.

'Morrison was an incredible talent with a complicated background. He was a difficult boy, a bit like Paul Gascoigne, if you see what I mean,' is all McGuinness will say. Born and brought up in Wythenshawe, one of Greater Manchester's trouble spots, Morrison was considered the brightest hope of the 1993 squad. 'This guy was the best young kid I've ever seen in my life,' Rio Ferdinand said recently, confirming that he was spotted by Alex Ferguson himself. A wasted talent. At 24, Morrison has a chequered history both on and off the pitch: United, West Ham, Birmingham, Queens Park Rangers and Lazio. Plenty of teams but no breakthrough. But back then, Ravel was top dog in the Under-18s. Everyone admired him and everyone tried to copy him. Even the new arrival admired him. And challenged him. 'Every day between Ravel and Paul was a challenge,' remembers McGuinness. 'They never stopped coming up with new tricks in training. They had an outlet for their need to overdo things in the playground session, where the kids are free to play however they want to, like in street football. We would mix the age groups, so Marcus Rashford, who was twelve at the time, played with Pogba and Morrison.' This challenge also continued on the pitch. 'If Ravel scored two goals in a match, you could be certain that the following week, Paul would do everything he could to get two of his own,' explains McGinty. They were enemies with the ball at their feet but friends off the pitch; Paul and Ravel shared the limelight. It was also thanks to them that the Under-18s topped Group C in the Premier Academy League and qualified for the play-off semi-final. On 7 May 2010, the Young Reds faced Arsenal at 11am. It finished 0–0 after 90 minutes. Extra time: Oğuzhan Özyakup, the Gunners' Turkish midfielder scored, followed by an equaliser from Cofie eleven minutes later. Penalties: 3–5, McGuinness's boys were eliminated. None of the players from the North London team missed; King, Wotton and Pogba scored for the Reds but Tunnicliffe misfired. Arsenal went on to win the league, beating Nottingham Forest in the final.

For United the season would end there, but for Paul Labile Pogba there was more to come. He was due to play in the Under-17 European Championships held in Liechtenstein from 18 to 30 May. 'It's always very good to get back with the French national team, to see all the players,' Paul told *UEFA.com*. 'We always speak together, joking, kidding, maybe seven in one room speaking and playing. It is a very good group, we are very happy in the team.' Paul also talked about his first eight months in Manchester during the interview and said of the first team: 'Sometimes I can see them, speak to them, joke, play table tennis. I am very close to them. Gabriel Obertan, because he's French, Patrice Evra and Rio Ferdinand, I can speak with him. He says good luck, just work hard. You have to be a good player. Sometimes they come and watch the games and try to help me. That's good, as they have a lot of experience. I listen to them and try to learn quickly.' One of the players he was keen to learn from was Paul Scholes: 'He's an example of how to train to

be the best. He was always there at the end of training, practising passes and shots. He never missed one,' Pogba would
later remember. Paul spied on the greats, trying to steal their
secrets, but at the same time he had become, for the younger
players, 'the Pied Piper. All his younger teammates tried to
copy him,' McGuinness recalled.

18 May 2010; France began their Euro Under-17 campaign against Spain. The French manager, Guy Ferrier, said:
'Pogba isn't playing because he isn't prepared physically or,
most importantly, mentally.' The Roja won 2–1. The second match was against Portugal. The *Bleuet*'s [Little Blues]
number 6 did what was expected of him and played his best
match of the year in a France shirt; a deflected shot from
him decided the match. France won 1–0 and, on beating
Switzerland three days later (3–1), qualified for the semi-
final. Their adventure came to an end against England at the
Rheinpark in Vaduz on 27 May. They were two goals down at
half time, both scored by Connor Wickham. In the 56th minute, Pogba seemed to put things back in doubt after scoring
a header on the end of a cross from Abdoulaye Doucouré,
but in the end the French fell at the hands of the English,
the eventual winners of the tournament.

'We lost but we learned. It was an experience that helped
me grow,' Paul would later claim.

Chapter 11

A Band of Brothers

Paul has just come home from a morning of golf. It rained, as it often does in Manchester, but he is unperturbed.

He removes his outer layers and explains: 'Nowadays they make waterproofs that keep you completely dry.' That may well be the case but the golf and the rain left their mark on another Paul. Seven years later, he would still remember it, telling *So Foot*: 'My host family would spend their time playing golf, even when it was raining.'

Carol and Paul Dalby are the family that welcomed Paul Pogba into their home in Manchester. Sitting in the kitchen of their new home they remember those years: 'When Jessica, our daughter, was fifteen she was at the Ashton-on-Mersey School. Manchester United are one of the school's sponsors and they were looking for English families to host foreign kids at the club. We decided to give it a try,' explains 59-year-old Carol, newly retired after a lifetime at Hewlett Packard. 'We lived in Sale, at 1, Edinburgh Close, near the training grounds.' She finds a picture on her phone of a small red-brick, two-storey house covered in snow. It almost looks like a Christmas card. 'The first boy we hosted was Davide Petrucci, from Rome, a Roma player; he was a pleasure to have in the house. The following year, Paul arrived.' 'He was a fun kid, always ready with a joke,' adds 60-year-old Paul, a former geography teacher, now working in the sports trophy business. 'His English wasn't great, but he tried. He could make you cry with laughter when he would put on airs and graces at the dinner table, carefully repeating every word "Please may I have a little more of this truly delicious ice cream."' Carol remembers: 'Every morning we would stick a post-it note on the fridge with a new word or phrase in English for them to learn that day. There would be a test in the evening. The two boys applied themselves and saw the results.' 'It was great fun to watch them teach each other swear words: one with the very worst of the Paris *banlieue* and the other how to let rip in Roman dialect.'

'Paul taught me French and I taught him Italian,' explains Petrucci, now a midfielder at Çaykur Rizespor, a Turkish team from Rize. 'We used to, no, we *do* get on well. Paul and I. He's a great guy, really nice, always positive. I've always enjoyed spending time with him. On the pitch, we were the two midfielders for the reserve team. Off the pitch, we would have dinner together and go to school to study English. We liked being at the Dalbys', they were a bit like our parents, our second family. Even now we're still in touch a lot. Paul has stayed in contact with them too.'

'That's true, he's always been so nice to us,' Paul Dalby remembers. 'He gave me the France shirt he wore when he played against England in the Under-17 Euros. And he invited us to Old Trafford on my 60th birthday. He scored in the 86th minute and came right to the bottom of the stand to dedicate the goal to me.' 'I hope he and Davide will be able to come to Jessica's wedding next year,' says Carol, showing a photo of a birthday party from years earlier, with her daughter and Paul, wearing a hat tilted jauntily to the side. A table laden with food at a central Manchester restaurant. 'It was frightening to see him eat,' Paul Dalby remembers. 'In the summer we would often have barbecues in the garden. Paul would pile his plate up with chicken and steak and then garnish it all with a single salad leaf. We would also invite the boy's teammates to the barbecues and we would always end up playing ping-pong: the golfers against the footballers. Paul was really fantastic with a bat and ball, but we didn't do too badly. They were a great group, Paul and his teammates. They really enjoyed those years.'

'The best thing,' recalls Michele Fornasier, 'was when we won the FA Youth Cup for Under-18 teams.' Paul McGuinness agrees: 'The 2010–11 season was crazy. Unforgettable. A fantastic experience for the boys who grew up together and gained in confidence game after game. For them, it was almost a simulation of the situations faced by the first team every week. Step-by-step, they overcame difficulties, tension, the nerves that go with playing in big stadiums like Anfield, Stamford Bridge, Old Trafford, in an environment that can sometimes be hostile, in front of fans, who, in the case of the final in Sheffield, were 30,000 strong, more than they had seen all year. That Under-18 team wasn't a team but a band of brothers. Speaking of Paul, I remember he made his debut in the reserves against Bolton (2 November 2010, Manchester United–Bolton Wanderers, 3–1). Ferguson had called him up in February for an FA Cup game (19 February 2011, Manchester United–Crawley Town, 1–0). He didn't start. He stayed on the bench but he got his first team number: 42. Paul trained with the reserves but came with us for cup games.'

For United, one of the tournament's favourites, the FA Youth Cup began against Portsmouth. All United's top brass were in attendance in the stands at Altrincham's Moss Lane ground: Fergie, Sir Bobby Charlton and David Gill, the chief executive. After half an hour of play, with the score at 0–0, the ball arrived at the feet of the young French player 25 yards from goal. Without hesitation, he fired the ball with his right foot. Tom Fry, the Pompey Youth's keeper, had nowhere to go. It hit the back of the net. The final result was 3–2 to the Red Devils. Everyone was talking about the number 8's wonder strike. Their cup run began well and continued in the same vein. United knocked out West Ham (1–0), Newcastle (1–0) and, in the quarter-final, faced Liverpool at Anfield on 14 March.

It was a match that had everything, including four red cards. One of those was shown to Paul Pogba. United were two goals down thanks to Adam Morgan. Stephen Sama brought down Ryan Tunnicliffe in the area in the 58th minute, Red card. Penalty. Pogba stepped up to take it. He scored but the goal was disallowed and the French player received a second yellow card, followed by a red. David Coote, the referee, judged his run-up as 'unsporting'. The French player had done what the Brazilians call a *paradinha*, a little stop halfway through his run-up. Although he may have exaggerated a bit, the referee's decision was bizarre. Larnell Cole took it upon himself to score the re-taken penalty and then the flawed genius Ravel Morrison scored twice to make sure of the result. 3–2 to United and McGuinness's boys were into the semi-final. This time against Chelsea. The first leg was played at Stamford Bridge on Sunday 10 April 2011. Nathaniel Chalobah, the Blues' number 4, took his team to 2–0. Jesse Lingard put United back in contention from a corner kick. 2–1. The Blues stretched their lead again thanks to Bobby Devine, but Pogba gave Man U fresh hope. The young French player showed what he was made of in the 55th minute: he got past two opponents with a roulette worthy of Zidane before unleashing a powerful shot from 25 yards out that grazed the crossbar. He had been unlucky and would be again with his follow-up shot that was cleared off the line by Jamal Blackman, the last line of the Chelsea defence. Finally, he would have something to celebrate: on the end of a cross from Lingard on the right, the number 8 jumped higher than everyone else and headed the ball into the opposite corner. 3–2 to the Blues, right under the nose of the club's owner Roman Abramovich. In the return leg at Old Trafford on 20 April, United overwhelmed the Blues with a hat trick from Will Keane and an opening goal from Ravel Morrison, booking their place in the final against Sheffield United.

The first leg was played at Bramall Lane on 17 May in a fantastic atmosphere. The crowd were keen to see a great game and United's latest young star, although the home team did not disappoint. Jesse Lingard had three opportunities within the space of a minute. The last and most contentious was the one that succeeded. A cross from Pogba came in from the right but despite pressure from a defender the Red Devils' number 7 got his foot on the ball that struck the keeper as he came out of his goal, flew up and went in under the crossbar. It looked as if Harry Maguire had used his hand to redirect the ball. In or out? The referee Michael Oliver gave the goal! Lingard couldn't believe it but it was 1–0 to United. Kyle McFadzean made things even with an incredible slingshot from just outside the centre circle.

There was more to come: Pogba to Lingard, a cross from Lingard and Will Keane made it 2–1. But the lead was short-lived: Jordan Slew, the home team's number 10, shot from the edge of the area. The ball took a deflection from Thorpe and, to the delight of the 30,000 in attendance, flew past Johnstone: 2–2. There would be all to play for in the return leg at the Theatre of Dreams. Monday 23 May 2011. The day after the big boys had won the Premier League and brought home the nineteenth league title in United's history, the youngsters in red beat Sheffield United 4–1 to win the FA Youth Cup. It was the Red Devils' tenth since the competition had begun in 1953. No English club had won more. There were two men of the match: Ravel Morrison, who opened the scoring and scored again to make it 3–0 (his sixth goal of the tournament) and Will Keane, the number 9, who also scored two, a penalty and a low shot to put the game out of the Sheffield team's reach. The boys celebrated by lifting the cup under the watchful eye of Sir Alex and the 23,000 fans in attendance. Three of the key players in the team had their photo taken in the dressing room, sprawled across the bench against the red-brick wall hung with white towels: Paul Pogba, the tallest, is in the middle, offering a tired smile, his thumbs are up in victory and his long arms stretched out around the shoulders of his two friends. Lingard, on the right, is holding the cup; Morrison, on the left, is leaning into the shot. There was no doubt they made a great team!

Chapter 12

Fergie's Biggest Mistake

'Pogba signed for Juventus a long time ago as far as we're aware. It's a bit disappointing because I don't think he showed us any respect at all. To be honest, if they carry on that way, I'm quite happy that he's away, from me, anyway.'

These were the words of a furious Sir Alex Ferguson as he angrily spoke to *MUTV* on 3 July 2012. Pogba's departure was a blow to the Scot, a defeat, a serious mistake for which he would still be blamed today. But how was it possible that the man who had spent 27 years on the United bench could have had the wool pulled over his eyes? How was it possible that the manager who had helped United become one of the richest clubs in the world could have allowed a player with such potential to escape for want of a handful of euros? How could the coach who had won so much (two Champions Leagues, two Cup Winners' Cups, two UEFA Super Cups, one Intercontinental Cup and one Club World Cup, not to mention fifteen domestic titles) have permitted a midfielder, who could have helped him win even more, to slip through his fingers? How could a proven talent scout like him (someone who, for example, took Cristiano Ronaldo from Sporting Lisbon at eighteen and gave him the number 7 shirt in the first team) have not held on tight to Pogba? The story is long and dramatic, with plenty of contradictory versions, surprises, rejections, wrong decisions, illusions and disappointments.

Where did it all begin? Let's go back to 19 September 2011. Sir Alex Ferguson, speaking at the unveiling of Manchester United's new commercial partner, Mister Potato, the Malaysian snack giant, announced that Pogba would start for the first team at Elland Road against Leeds United in the third round of the Carling Cup. The boy had taken a knock in the Reserves' 2–1 win against Rochdale. 'But it's not too bad, though. He should be able to play on Tuesday,' said the Old Trafford boss, revealing that for now he had no intention of sending the player out on loan to help him gain experience. 'Maybe next year that could be an option but we're definitely expecting him this season to stay with Manchester United.' The Red Devils' manager put an end to the speculation that spoke of interest from Burnley. He added: 'It's more difficult to loan a boy of eighteen who's come from France. We prefer to keep him with us until we find he's mature enough to possibly go on loan.'

After 45 minutes at Elland Road on 20 September, United were winning 3–0. Michael Owen, in his first match of the season, had scored two while Ryan Giggs got the third. It was as a substitute for the Welsh player that, at the beginning of the second half, Paul Pogba made his debut with the big boys. The TV commentators said: 'He is regarded like a rising star at Old Trafford. He is just eighteen, French, midfielder, a really competitive footballer.' He was not the only debutant: Larnell Cole and Zeki Fryers were also taking to the stage. Wearing the famous red shirt, black shorts and the number 42, Paul Pogba, with a slight Mohican, took his place in midfield. He showed focus and character. He did not hold back in tackles, picked up the ball, was on the receiving end of two bad fouls, won a free-kick, tried a couple of long shots and played until the end of the game. The two shots came from the edge of the area. He misjudged them both: one went well wide and the other ended up in the stands. But the overall verdict was positive. Paul received compliments from his teammates and his manager, who confirmed during the post-match press conference: 'Pogba had a good 45,' adding about the three boys: 'They did well. It's good for them to get a taste of the atmosphere and what the first team is like.'

At Carrington they had known for a while that Paul was ready for the first team. But Fergie was dragging his feet. The number 42's second opportunity did not come until 25 October, again in the Carling Cup, away to Aldershot, a League Two team. In the 60th minute, with the Red Devils 3–0 up, the Scot brought on Pogba in place of Tom Cleverley. Nine minutes later the number 42 tried a shot from the edge of the area. Boom. The ball flew over the crossbar. Next time. But it would be a month until the next time. Still in the Carling Cup, but this time at Old Trafford. It was 30 November and it could not have gone any worse: Crystal Palace knocked out United with a goal in extra time and went through to the semi-final. Pogba came on as a substitute for Rafael in the 63rd minute. He tried a shot from outside the area but it was off target. The boy returned to the Reserves, where he was not short of goals, success and satisfaction. At the end of the season, United won the Premier Reserve League on penalties in the play-off final against Aston Villa; they were victorious in the Manchester Senior Cup beating City 2–0 in the Etihad Stadium and also won the Lancashire Cup. But it was not the stuff of which Paul Pogba's dreams were made. The young French player wanted to show what he could do with the big boys in the Premier League. He was frustrated by the choices of his manager. He felt that he was not taking him into consideration and underestimated him. Breaking point eventually came, a point of no return in the relationship between Paul and

Ferguson, between United and the Frenchman. Or at least that was how Pogba saw it. On Saturday 31 December 2011, Sir Alex was celebrating his 70th birthday. Blackburn Rovers, who were bottom of the table, came to Old Trafford. 'Paul Scholes had retired. Darren Fletcher was injured. There was no one left to play in midfield. And I was training and I was beginning to get better bit by bit. The coach never stopped telling me "You're this far." And I didn't understand. This far from what? Playing? From having some playing time? From getting on the field? Or what?' Pogba told *Canal+* in 2014. 'And there was Rafael in midfield and I was disgusted, I didn't get on the field for the whole game. I lost the relationship I had with the manager and I was really disappointed.'

La Pioche was convinced he would be in the starting eleven given all the injury problems. But Fergie instead chose to put Carrick in the centre of the defence and give room in the midfield to Rafael and Park Ji-sung. Pogba ended up on the bench and in the second half it was Anderson who took Chicharito's place when he left the field. The match ended with a historic defeat (3–2 to Rovers) and Pogba had reached boiling point. Ferguson tried to calm him down, telling him he needed time to break through into the Premier League, asking him to be patient as Scholes and Giggs had been, but Pogba was not listening. He did not want to wait, he wanted to play. And when, at the beginning of January, he heard that Scholesy had agreed to come out of retirement, he thought his chances had been reduced even further. He admired the 37-year-old midfielder, who had hung up his boots six months earlier, but he knew that his return to the game would see him slip even further down the list of eligible midfielders.

Paul's long-awaited Premier League debut came on 31 January 2012 in a home game against Stoke, but it only lasted a handful of minutes. He made three more appearances in March, all starting on the bench: against West Brom and Wolves in the league, and Athletic Bilbao in the Europa League. The match in which the Red Devils were knocked out by the Basques.

'You're at United, but you're not playing. Perhaps you'd be better off looking for a chance somewhere else,' said his brother, Mathias. The entire clan led by Yeo Moriba came together when faced with the impatience shown by Sir Alex's club at getting the boy to renew his contract. The three-year contract that Paul had signed in 2009 expired in 2012; he had the option of renewing it for a further year, but, at the behest of Oualid Tanazefti, Carmine 'Mino' Raiola got involved. The Dutch-Italian agent of Balotelli and Ibrahimović, the man had a good nose for promising young players and lucrative deals.

'There are one or two football agents I simply do not like, and Mino Raiola is one of them. I distrusted him from the moment I met him. Our first meeting was a fiasco. He and I were like oil and water. From then our goose was cooked because Raiola had been able to ingratiate himself with Paul and his family and the player signed with Juventus,' the Scot would say in his latest book, *Leading*. This differs from the version Raiola gave the *Financial Times* in 2016:

'Ferguson to Raiola: "I don't talk to you if the player is not here."

Raiola: "Get the player out of the locker room and sit him here." Pogba enters.

Ferguson to Pogba: "You don't want to sign this contract?"

Pogba: "We're not going to sign this contract under these conditions."

Ferguson to Raiola: "You're a twat."

Raiola: "This is an offer that my chihuahuas – I have two chihuahuas – don't sign."

Ferguson: "What do you think he needs to earn?"

Raiola: "Not that."

Ferguson: "You're a twat."'

The deal had stalled, for financial reasons: Raiola & Co had requested £15,000 a week. The salary of a first team player, which, according to United, Pogba was not yet. Nor would the club guarantee the number of minutes Paul would play next season. The two sides' positions were very far apart. Ferguson would try again to convince the boy and his entourage.

He sent in Patrice Evra, the player's friend and a father figure to him. But to no avail. The Scot took the situation in hand. 'He came to my house on his own. We were all there, with his brothers, and we decided Paul would not renew his contract with United. Ferguson', Yeo Moriba told *AFP*, 'punished him because of that and wouldn't let him play.' 'They left me out because they said I wanted to leave,' the French player told the *BBC*. 'That is disrespect.'

Yeo added: 'At that moment Paul was on his own. He even ended up crying in the manager's office because of how he had been treated.' There was no doubt that the boy was unhappy; he could not sleep and was having a tough time, pulled from one side to the other by a desire to stay, but also wanting to leave.

Paul swore he loved Manchester and United, but Bayern Munich, Real Madrid and PSG, according to Oualid Tanazefti in 2016, were all courting him. There were others as well: Raiola was knocking on the doors of clubs in Italy. Mino had a great relationship with Adriano Galliani, the CEO of AC Milan. At Juventus, one of his former charges, Pavel Nedved, the Czech 2003 Ballon d'Or winner, now had a seat on the Old Lady's board. The *rossoneri* seemed interested but Juve really had the boy in their sights. Pogba flew to Turin and hit it off with Antonio Conte, the Juventus manager. 'Don't go to Italy, there's racism there,' Ferguson is said to have told him to put him off. Even Raiola, or so they say, apparently laid the difficulties he would face as a young player in the Bel Paese on the table for him. Pogba was unsure, thinking it would be a backward step, but eventually signed for Juventus. It was the end, or at least for the time being, of his love story with United. And that brings us back to Sir Alex's anger on 3 July 2012.

They were eating their hearts out in Manchester at having lost such a gem of a player; years later they would find out exactly how much the Scot's big mistake had cost the club. In Turin they were rubbing their hands with glee. For next to nothing (Juventus would pay United €1 million), they had taken home 'the new Vieira and the fake Balotelli,' according to *La Gazzetta dello Sport.* The boy introduced himself to *Sky Sports*: 'I'm a technical player, despite how tall I am. I'm good at shooting but I like being on the ball. I take my inspiration from Vieira and everyone tells me I'm a lot like him. Physically, I've been mistaken for Balotelli. But I think I look more like Mario's brother.'

Chapter 13

Juventus Tour

The red bus pulls out of Park 7 at the Juventus Stadium at 3.31pm. With the sun at its hottest, there are few people about on such a warm afternoon. It is clearly not a match day – there are only a handful of customers for the Juventus City Tour. Those who are there are undeterred and have already bought their €25 tickets from the driver. Paola, a blonde sporting a red tie, an employee of City Sightseeing Torino, provides tourists with red headphones to listen to the commentary (in Italian only, for now), plus a card with photos of the city on both sides.

The Juventus Stadium – a silver spaceship complete with three gold stars to symbolise the *bianconeri*'s 33 league titles, and a black and white heart – is now behind them. Stefano, wearing the club strip – with a freshly cut beard, Juventus bracelets and the gift of the gab – begins his spiel. He is the guide provided by the *Vecchia Signora* and he will more than two hours talking about various symbolic sites in the history of the *bianconeri*. To add some light relief, Paola will talk about Turin's monuments, squares, palaces, elegant cafés and curiosities.

The J-Stadium is the first topic. Between the Vallette and Lucento neighbourhoods, this part of town was once home to the Stadio Delle Alpi, built for the Italia 90 World Cup. It had a short life; too large and too expensive, it also had serious structural problems. In 2002, Juventus, who had long been harbouring the idea of a stadium all of their own, signed an agreement with the City of Turin granting them the rights to the Delle Alpi site for 99 years. In 2008, work began to demolish the World Cup stadium. Three years later, on 8 September 2011, to coincide with the celebrations for the 150th anniversary of Italian Unification, the Juventus Stadium was inaugurated. The event was marked by an official ceremony and a friendly against Notts County, a name that will reappear in the history of the Turin club.

The bus travels along the avenues of Italy's fourth largest city in terms of inhabitants. Born as a Roman *castrum*, it went on to become the seat of the former ruling Savoy family, who accentuated its military appearance. Turin is a city built on a lattice of straight streets; in the twentieth century, the industrial city, the city of the automobile and of Fiat, was grafted on to this urban structure.

Corso Galileo Ferraris, 32: a serious and dignified building, like the city itself, is the current headquarters of Juventus FC SpA. After a quick glance, the tour continues along Corso Re Umberto. There's a story here. On a bench on Corso Re Umberto, one of the elegant avenues of central Turin, a group of students from the nearby Ginnasio Liceo Classico Massimo D'Azeglio school came together to chat and discuss the new sport that had just been imported from England: football. An idea was forming in their heads: why not start a sports club? On 1 November 1897, the Sport Club Juventus was born. Few people were keen on the name, preferring Società Via Fort or Società Polisportiva Massimo d'Azeglio. In the end the Juventus supporters had their way. The first president was Enrico Canfari, who had a mechanic's workshop at Corso Re Umberto, 42 with his brother Eugenio. It was the club's first headquarters. Their first pitch was in Piazza d'Armi. Their first strip was pink with a little black tie. The father of one of the members was in the textile industry and gave the boys a piece of pink percale. The colour was not really ideal but given the lack of funds in the club's coffers they could hardly turn up their noses. In 1899, the club changed its name to Football Club Juventus. A year later, on 11 March 1900, Juventus played their first official match in the national football league. They lost 1–0 to FC Torinese. The black and white stripes arrived in 1903. The story goes that the club asked Tom Gordon Savage, also known as John, an English footballer based in Turin, to obtain a more professional looking playing uniform. Savage turned to a manufacturer in his home town, Nottingham, who decided to make life easy and sent whatever they had in the warehouse: a stock of shirts with black and white vertical stripes. In short, it was the strip worn by Notts County, one of the world's oldest clubs (founded in 1862) and the second team in the city behind Nottingham Forest. The Juve members and players were not keen on the black and white but in the end they had to give in when the order arrived: English shirts were the utmost in professionalism after all so they resigned themselves to it. 1905: Juventus won their first league title on 9 April ahead of Genova and Milanese. 2017: the Old Lady won its 33rd Italian title on 21 May.

Porta Nuova, the nineteenth-century station recently returned to its former glory, and Via Roma, pure fascist architecture. Paola turns to point out the tobacconist under the porticoes where Marcello Lippi, one of Juve's most decorated managers, would order his cigars. The enormous white statues of a man and a woman representing the Po and the Dora, the two rivers that run through Turin, lead into Piazza San Carlo. But the bus is prohibited from following and the card distributed at the start of the tour comes into its own: the city's so-called 'living room', where the *bianconeri* fans celebrate titles, can be admired from a photograph. As can the exquisite Galleria San Federico, home to one of Juventus's earliest headquarters.

Piazza Castello, the heart of the city. And next, Palazzo Madama, a World Heritage site with two distinctly different faces – a Baroque façade on one side and a medieval castle on the other – home to the Civic Museum of Ancient Art. Its gardens, towers, staircases and rooms also contain the complete history of the city, from the Roman period to the Risorgimento.

A little further on stands the Palazzo Reale, home to the treasures of the House of Savoy, and the nearby Egyptian Museum, one of the world's greatest collections of ancient Egyptian masterpieces.

The bus turns into Via Po, a long road that leads down to the river alongside uninterrupted porticoes built on the left because the Savoy family and the Torinese nobility were not keen on braving the rain when out strolling. Piazza Vittoria Veneto, enormous and elegant. Then behind, above the roofs, the tip of the Mole Antonelliana, originally a synagogue, now home to the Cinema Museum. It is the symbol of the city that can be found in a thousand different variations in Turin's souvenir shops. For more than a century, the Mole, at 167.5 metres, was the city's tallest building, although it has now been overtaken by the Piedmont Region skyscraper (209 metres) and reached, but not surpassed, out of respect, by the new Intesa San Paolo banking group skyscraper (167 metres and 25 centimetres).

This beautiful, slender building was designed by Renzo Piano but cannot compete with the Alpine peaks that provide the city with its backdrop on clear days.

Beyond the Po loom the hill and dome of the Gran Madre, a church built on the model of the Pantheon that provides a good example of Turin's dark side. Apparently it is the geographical intersection between the triangle of black magic and white magic, according to specialists in occultism. Mystery reigns in these parts. For example, fans of esotericism claim that the statue of Faith at the Gran Madre stands on the exact spot where the Holy Grail is buried.

On to the Vittorio Emanuele Bridge, with picture perfect views to the right of the Monte dei Cappuccini, home to the Mountain Museum. In the distance, raised up on the left, the Basilica of Superga, a Baroque explosion by Filippo Juvarra and one that is synonymous with tragedy. On 4 May 1949, the plane bringing home the Torino team crashed into a retaining wall at the back of the Basilica of Superga. The accident resulted in the deaths of the entire team that had won five consecutive league titles and was the backbone of the Italian national team. It was not just the players who died but also the club's directors, support staff and journalists who had been attending a friendly against Benfica in Lisbon.

Corso Moncalieri, along the Po. Stefano points out Da Angelino, a restaurant beloved of Giampiero Boniperti, captain of the *bianconeri* in the 1940s and 50s then president of Juve from 1971 to 1990. A few hundred metres further on, the nightclub where the Juve team celebrates its victories appears. In the centre of Piazza Crimea a truncated obelisk and sculptural group remembers the expeditionary force sent, in 1855, by what was then the Kingdom of Sardinia to fight in the Crimean War against the Russian Empire. It is one of many monuments that dot the squares of the city centre. Kings and generals, infantrymen and tommies, unknown soldiers and horsemen, the entire nineteenth-century history of the Kingdom of Savoy and the Kingdom of Italy cast here in bronze and white marble. Amidst the green on the other side of the river stands the Castello del Valentino and park where, some one hundred years ago, a handful of well-to-do young men began kicking a ball around. Boats swarm the river; the sunny weather favours another of the Torinesi's passions: rowing.

The Stadio Olimpico Grande Torino comes into view. It has had many different names over the years. In 1933, when it was inaugurated, just a year before the 1934 World Cup, it was named after Benito Mussolini in honour of the fascist leader. After the Second World War, it became the Stadio Comunale. It was Juve's ground until the early 1960s, when Torino left the old Stadio Filadelfia. Both teams played there for almost 30 years until the opening of the Stadio Delle Alpi. It was still not the end and the reshaped and radically restructured Comunale became the Stadio Olimpico, host of the opening and closing ceremonies of the twentieth Winter Olympics held in Turin and the mountains of Piedmont. The year 2006 marked a turning point in the city's development, metamorphosis and change. During the 1980s, Turin suffered like Detroit during the crisis in the automobile industry; the wheels were starting to come off the great factory town that had survived for a hundred years. The Fiat factories fired thousands and thousands of workers. The working class lost its final battle. Production facilities were relocated all over the world. The industrial and manufacturing context of the 1950s and 1960s, which saw the largest ever internal migration from the south to the north, the foundation of the economic boom and the struggle for workers' rights, was radically changing. In order to overcome the crisis, Turin focused on research, knowledge, the arts, culture and its historic heritage. Thanks also to the momentum of the Olympic Games, the city was given a new look, rediscovered its centre, with its elegant eighteenth-century palaces, and found a new impetus. It was a shame that the city was divided: downtown and suburbs, two distinct environments on a collision course.

Talking of suburbs and Fiat, here we are at the Mirafiori plant, the largest industrial complex in Italy: three million square metres, 22 kilometres of internal roads, and 70,000 ancillary and service workers in the 1970s. There are now 17,000.

The central building is located at 200, Corso Giovanni Agnelli, built from white Pietra di Finale stone. A yellow Fiat 500 sits outside, with a red one inside. The shields of the Fiat Chrysler Automobiles Group's brands are mounted on the façade: Abarth, Lancia, Fiat, Alfa Romeo and Jeep.

After the factory come the meadows: grazing cows and a flock of sheep moving down a side street. The road climbs: at crossroads and roundabouts prostitutes await late afternoon clients, further on old farms have been converted into restaurants. Finally, the two white wings of the main building of the Palazzina di Caccia di Stupinigi. The House of Savoy's hunting lodge, entertainment and wedding venue, it was built to a Juvarra design from 1729. Even from the moving bus it is impossible not to spot the enormous bronze deer on the dome of the central building. But mere deer were not enough for the House of Savoy. The palace was also home to Fritz, an Indian elephant received by King Carlo Felice in 1827 as a gift from Muhammad Ali, Viceroy of Egypt. He was the menagerie's main attraction for years.

And here we are at the penultimate stop on our tour: Vinovo. Among the green wheat fields, we can make out a grey and white rectangular building: the Juventus Training Centre (English is thrown around in these parts nowadays just as French once was among the Torinese nobility). It stands on what used to be the Vinovo race course. Despite having lost some of its features, the hippodrome has retained its sand trotting ring on the other side of the road. Racing unfortunately stopped some time ago. For the *bianconeri* fans, waiting for their idols to come crashing through the door, watching the horses racing would have been a good way of killing time. The horses, drivers and their sulkies are easy to spot from the Juventus Training Centre but nothing of the first team training pitches can be seen from the red bus. These are protected by a high green hedge.

Viale Torino and Corso Unione Sovietica, then the bus turns for home. The landscape is not particularly exciting. Paola entertains the tourists with the gastronomy of Piedmont. She explains its typical dishes: from *vitello tonnato* to *bicherin*, from *agnolotti* with roast meat sauce to *fritto misto*, from *ravioli del plin* to *bagna cauda*, with *bonet* and *amaretto* peaches for dessert. It's enough to gladden a hungry tourist's stomach. What follows is instead food for the fans' soul: Juventus's four club songs. Singing is encouraged: 'Juve, a story of a great white love embracing black. A choir that sings for you.' As the final notes ring out the bus circles the J-Stadium. It returns to its departure point. Stefano points out the farmstead undergoing renovation that will become the club's new headquarters. It will be part of the J-Village, which will be home to six new facilities: the new first team training centre with an annexed media centre, the J-Hotel, the World International School and a new concept store.

With thanks for the tour and the commentary, the tourists say goodbye and get off the bus. It is 5.50pm, time to end an afternoon of full *bianconero* immersion with a bang. Firstly, with a stroll along the stars' walk (the Juventus version of the Walk of Fame), which pays tribute with large gold stars to the team's greatest players and with silver stars to the 39 victims of the Heysel Stadium tragedy. This is followed by a visit to the J-Museum, 1,500 square metres that tell of 120 years of history through memorabilia, trophies, shirts, balls, holograms and videos.

A sinuous yellow line guides visitors through the black walls and floors. This is the goal zone: home to images of the club's greatest goals. Here we find Zizou, King David (Trezeguet), Nedved, Bettega, Del Piero, Thuram, Platini and Sívori. One phenomenon after another. Then the sacred temple of the *bianconero* liturgy: the trophy room. Gold and silver sparkle in the darkness; two Venetian guys go crazy filming everything, absolutely everything, on their smartphones, including video clips of matches that recall who, where, how and when Juventus won the Champions League, the Intercontinental Cup, league titles, the UEFA Cup and the Italian Super Cup ... Outside the temple, a panel tells the story of the Agnelli family with hearsay and quotes; this is the saga of the presidents of Juventus, part of the club's DNA. Omar Sívori, the Italo-Argentine 1961 Ballon d'Or winner, says: 'Juve gets into your blood because it's about style, class and seriousness. No other team in Italy knows how to win as much or in the way they do. The *scudetto* is only celebrated for a night because they're already thinking about the next one.' Next up is Zinédine Zidane, who won the Ballon d'Or in 1998: 'I learned the winning mentality at Juve. It was only there that I grasped that winning is an obligation. To be part of one of the biggest clubs in the world makes you understand the importance of the result.'

In the main room history is on the right. It begins with a 'Once upon a time in 1897' before twisting and turning through panels, photographs, memorabilia and enlarged pictures. This is history with a capital H, that of the club and its sporting eras, victories and stars: from John Charles to Sívori to Michel Platini, the French player beloved of Giovanni Agnelli, to Pinturicchio and Buffon. A Tuscan schoolgirl and kids wearing orange caps and matching backpacks are wary of the myriad of written panels; they prefer to rush up to the screens where they can choose the match clips they want to watch. On the left, a small group of elderly gentlemen with their noses in the air admire the glass cases containing the shirts of players who have exceeded 300 appearances for the team. Starting with Chiellini and finishing with Alessandro Del Piero, number 10, 705 appearances from 1993 to 2012. The parade of those who have made the club's history is impressive. Here's shirt number 17, which belonged to David Sergio Trezeguet, 320 appearances from 2000 to 2011, with 171 goals, an outright record for a foreigner in the *bianconero* team. A little further on the Old Lady's Ballons d'Or. Of course, Platini, the Sun King, is there, three times winner of the *France Football* award. The love story between the *Vecchia Signora* and Michel lasted for five long years from 1982 to 17 May 1987, when, at age 32, he decided that ageing on the football pitch was not for him. He left without a fuss, having made 224 appearances and scored 104 goals for the club. In a cabinet his number 10 shirt hangs beneath that of Sívori, the rebel angel. A girl carefully reads the memorial with the names of the Heysel victims as her boyfriend negotiates cardboard cut-outs of a certain Gigi Buffon. Then into the third to last room, filled with 360 degree images and a panel heralding: 'We are Juve. Eleven million fans in Italy, 300 million fans all over the world, 41 million fans in Europe.' A sentence spoken by Giovanni Agnelli dominating the entrance springs to mind: 'After a century of history [Juve] has become a legend, with a name, colours and a shirt known all over the world.'

It is into this team, into this history, that a nineteen year old named Paul Labile Pogba lands in the summer of 2012.

Making his debut for Manchester United against Leeds United in the Carling Cup at Elland Road, 20 September 2011
Phil Oldham/REX/Shutterstock

Celebrating scoring his first goal for Juventus against Napoli, 20 October 2012
Di Marco/Epa/REX/Shutterstock

Tussling with Lionel Messi of Barcelona in the UEFA Champions League Final in Berlin, 6 June 2015

Olycom SPA/ REX/Shutterstock

Pogba, Juan Cuadrado and Patrice Evra celebrate winning the Coppa Italia Final, 21 May 2016

Ciambelli/SIPA/REX/Shutterstock

Paul's brothers cheer him on during the UEFA Euro 2016 Final, 10 July 2016
Kieran McManus/BPI/REX/Shutterstock

Pogba cuts a dejected figure as Portugal celebrate Eder's winning goal
in the Euro 2016 Final, 10 July 2016
Joe Meredith/JMP/REX/Shutterstock

Pogba celebrates winning the EFL Cup Final against Southampton with a trademark Dab, 26 February 2017
Matt McNulty/JMP/REX/Shutterstock

Kissing the UEFA Europa League trophy after beating Ajax in the final in Stockholm, 24 May 2017
Peter Powell/EPA/REX/Shutterstock

Chapter 14

Shooooooooot!

Via Filadelfia 106, a 1950s red brick building with green shutters. Rising up into a triangular tower, it stretches as far as Corso Giovanni Agnelli. It was here, in an apartment on the seventh floor, that Paul Pogba lived when he arrived in Turin from Manchester. It was a strange choice: Juventus players, if they have families, kids and dogs, prefer villas in the hills; if they're single, they choose the city centre with its elegant eighteenth-century buildings. Here, however, we are in the Santa Rita district, an area that would once have been described as middle class. To get to Piazza San Carlo by car, it takes a good twenty minutes, depending on the traffic. But that's not all: the building is less than a hundred metres from the Stadio Olimpico Grande Torino, home to Torino, Juventus's biggest rivals. Cross a wide tree-lined avenue (Corso Giovanni Agnelli), busy with trams and multiple traffic lanes, and you will find yourself in front of one of the stadium gates.

These were odd coincidences for the French kid who would become the darling of the *bianconeri* fans. His neighbours remember him as a polite and decent guy, a good tenant who helped the elderly lady on the sixth floor carry up her shopping bags. 'It is true that sometimes after a win his friends would make a racket downstairs in the middle of the night,' says one lady, who, for the love of God does not want her name to appear, 'but he would put his head out of the window and tell them to stop, and they did.' But as well as the noise and 'lights on at all hours (I suffer from insomnia, you know!)', there is one episode the lady has not forgotten. 'I had given my parking space to a former colleague from school. One morning she called me and said she'd found it occupied by a big car, a Bentley or a Porsche or something, I wouldn't know. I went down and it didn't take me long to work out who the car belonged to. I rang the bell for the seventh floor. Paul Pogba came down with his girlfriend. My friend and I speak French, I taught it at school. "*Cette place, c'est à moi !*" [That's my space!], I shouted at him. He explained by saying he had lost the keys to his garage. "*Je m'en fous !*" [I don't care!], I replied.'

It must have made for quite a scene: two little old ladies verbally abusing a big guy, 6 foot 2 and 13 stone, and scolding him as if he were a schoolboy who had pulled a prank. 'The player', according to the lady, felt terrible about it, lowered his head, apologised and 'never parked his car in my space again'. Years later, worse things would happen to Pogba in this building. While he was playing at the San Siro, thieves cleaned out his apartment, taking jewellery and designer clothes. Nasty surprises aside, Pogba lived happily in this neighbourhood. There were plenty of shops and even a kebab house for when he didn't have time or didn't want to cook. All he had to do was take the lift down to the ground floor, leave through the green front door, cross the street and visit Olimpico Pizza Kebab, run by the three Oner brothers, at number 113, Via Filadelfia. The brothers now proudly show off photos with Paul and his ever-changing looks, or in the company of Uncle Pat Evra. They also remember that Pogba liked his kebabs extra spicy, with lots of meat and mozzarella, or a pizza kebab to take away.

Paul arrived in Turin on 26 July 2012. He was late because

he had taken a few days holiday after playing, with the captain's armband, in the Under-19 European Championships. It had been a great experience that came to an end in the semi-final, in the A. Le Coq Arena in Tallinn, against Spain. It was 3–3 after extra time and ended 4–2 to the Spaniards on penalties. The Roja won the title and the Bleuets went home empty handed. 'We had a good Euros, even if we lost to the Spanish on penalties. Paul was one of the leaders of the team both on the pitch and in the dressing room,' remembers Pierre Mankowski, the manager. 'He was very dynamic on the pitch. Against Serbia, in the first match, he scored a penalty to make it 2–0. He had a great match against Spain. He made it 3–3 in the 117th minute on the end of a cross from Digne. He took the first penalty and scored to give us the lead. But then luck wasn't on our side.' It had been a good journey for Pogba and a great introduction to Antonio Conte and Juventus. At 2.50pm on 27 July 2012, the talented French player finished his customary medical in Turin. He had been pronounced fit and able by his new club. All that was missing was for him to sign a contract that would tie him to the *Vecchia Signora* for four years (with a salary just short of €1.5 million) and the formalisation of the purchase. This would take place on 3 August at the club's headquarters on Corso Galileo Ferraris. To the right of the French midfielder, proudly showing off a Juventus shirt, Oualid Tanazefti, his first mentor, and, on his left, called into the scene by Pogba himself, his new agent, Mino Raiola. Photos, handshakes, jokes from the Dutch-Italian agent at the expense of Tanazefti and official declarations of the new purchase: 'I'm very happy with this new path I'm about to take. I hope to have a great season. In Manchester, I learned from champions such as Scholes, Rio Ferdinand and Rooney. I'm sure it'll be the same at Juve with Pirlo.'

Of course, Andrea Pirlo, the first to realise that the boy was strong and skinny but with legs that could get everywhere. 'They would have been mad to send him to the youth team. He had to stay with us. I remember on Pogba's first day of training we burst out laughing. We couldn't believe that a club as important as Manchester United would allow such a talented young player to leave on a free transfer,' remembers the linchpin of the New York City FC team. 'After the training session, I was going back to the dressing room when Buffon came over, laughing, and said: "Andrea, did they really let him leave for free?"'

Paul remembers his first day at Vinovo rather differently. 'I lost three kilos in my first training session,' the French player claimed. 'They worked hard at Juve, on fitness and tactics. In England training is more explosive and you don't stop much, but the tactics aren't the same and training sessions in Italy are longer.'

Four days of training and the new arrival 'went straight into the first team because he was already ready for the highest level,' said Beppe Marotta, the *bianconero* CEO.

Geneva, 1 August 2012. Juventus, champions of Italy, faced Benfica in a friendly. In the 78th minute, Conte understood he had a potential superstar on his hands, paying attention when Pirlo returned to the bench and sending the French kid on for the number 21. Paul Pogba made his debut. In those few minutes, during which the Serbian player Miloš Krasić cancelled out the goal scored by the Paraguayan Óscar Cardozo, he made a good impression. The French player set himself up in front of the defence and, with the odd perfectly measured pass, showed he had the right skills and the right character: he did not retreat when an opponent needed to be challenged. Both the bench and the stands were happy.

Paul Labile Pogba wore the number 6, which is sacred to Juventus fans. It was worn by Gaetano Scirea, an out-and-out sweeper who racked up 552 appearances for the team. He was a gentleman footballer who had won everything there was to win with Juve and the Italian national team but was tragically killed at the age of 36 in a road accident in Poland on his way home from a scouting mission to one of Juve's UEFA Cup opponents.

Pogba may have worn the number 6 but he was the fifteenth French player to pull on the famous *bianconero* shirt. In addition to the unforgettable Platini, Zidane and Trezeguet, Didier Deschamps (both as player and coach), Patrick Vieira, Thierry Henry, Jonathan Zebina, Jean-Alain Boumsong, Olivier Kapo and Armand Traoré had also spent time at the club, as would Nicolas Anelka, Patrice Evra and Kingsley Coman. The close relationship between France and Turin is built on history, climate, lifestyle and deliberately chosen affinities. The flow of players has continued uninterrupted since the early twentieth century. Was there a difference between Pogba and people such as Platini, Zidane and Trezeguet? Yes, and it was simple. Paul arrived at Juve when he was just nineteen. Michel was 27, Zizou, 24 and David, 23. He was an emerging footballer but one who looked very promising indeed. This was clear during the Berlusconi Trophy match on 19 August, when the *bianconeri* won their second title of the season beating Massimiliano Allegri's AC Milan 3–2. Juve had won the Italian Super Cup in Beijing, putting four goals past Napoli. But Pogba had not been part of the trip to China. At the San Siro, he seemed like a veteran, however. He played from the kick-off and lit up Juve with passes and wrong-footing turns. He was on the receiving end of applause from the Juve stands and positive reviews from the press. It was not just his football but the boy's maturity that impressed.

Guido Vaciago, a journalist with *Tuttosport*, a sport daily from Turin, remembers: 'He nutmegged Massimo Ambrosini who then cut him down in the next move. As if he was saying: I've won the Champions League, league titles and have I don't know how many Serie A appearances – you can't nutmeg me, kid! Pogba took it, got up and then returned the favour to the Milan player a few minutes later. To me it didn't seem like bravado but rather that Paul had bags of personality. By going in hard on his opponent he was saying that he respected him but that he deserved respect too because he was a footballer as well.'

The boy with bags of personality made his Serie A debut on 22 September 2012 in a home game against Chievo. Pirlo was being rested on the bench and the pairing of Conte and Carrera lined up the Frenchman for his first start. When it came down to it, he had always been seen as Pirlo's deputy, as a future replacement for the player, although they did not have the same characteristics. At age nineteen, he did not have the same vision of the game as the Brescian, but he knew what to do with the ball at his feet, was a good sweeper and did not turn his nose up at moving forward and trying to score. Paul had plenty of work to do to reach the level of Pirlo, the brain of the national team. All this may have been true but the experiment worked. Juve registered their fourth win in a row in as many league games and Paul was rated satisfactory by the press. He had passed his first test.

On 2 October, still at home at the J-Stadium, he made his Champions League debut, but only by a matter of minutes (the French player came on for Vidal in the 84th minute) in a tough match against Shakhtar Donetsk that finished 1–1. In a top of the table clash against Napoli on 20 October, Paul again substituted Vidal, who had seemed invisible in recent matches. The nineteen year old came on in the 30th minute of the second half. Seven minutes later the number 6, this time in black strip, scored the match-winning goal. Giovinco tried a shot from outside the area that came back off Paolo Cannavaro; the loose ball fell for Pogba, who, without hesitation, struck it with his left foot despite being a naturally right-footed player. He connected with the ball perfectly and fired it into the lower left corner of De Sanctis's net. Accuracy and power: it was a great goal. After firing the ball into the back of the net, Paul ran towards the stand where his cousins were watching. He was proud of having scored in front of them. After the game, which took Juve to the top of the table, Paul played around with French and English as he talked about his first goal in Italy: 'I gave it a try and it went well. But it's just one goal, one football match, and I won't let it go to my head. I don't think this goal will change my life here at Juve. Even though I don't feel any pressure here and I'm not surprised by the faith Conte has had in me from the beginning, because I have faith in myself.'

The boy was convinced by his skills and his manager counted on him. With Pirlo, Vidal and Marchisio, Juve's midfield was the team's strength, the open secret of Conte's first *scudetto* for the club. Paul had been enlisted to take the place of Pirlo (aged 33) but there was still plenty of time before a changing of the guard. Conte was carving out a role for the boy as an attacking midfielder that fitted him like a glove. The French player was eventually called up with increasing regularity. On a tedious, rainy night on 31 October, Paul gave Juve a win with a header in the dying moments of the game against Bologna. It was the icing on the cake for the best player on the pitch. Paul was irrepressible and the absence of both Marchisio and Vidal went unnoticed. He hit the post in the first half but went one further in the 92nd minute, using his head on the end of a soft cross from Giovinco that came in from the left. His header could be a weakness but this time it did the trick.

Life in black and white was not always a bed of roses. Tardiness at training sessions was inexcusable. Once was forgiven but a second time did not go unpunished. Paul was late on 9 November and as a result was not picked for the away match against Pescara the following day.

'I made a mistake. And I'm really sorry about it. And of course I'd like to apologise because I know it showed a lack of respect to Conte and my teammates,' he said in a long interview with *Tuttosport*. 'I didn't mean to do it and if I'm late it's because of very trivial reasons but it's still a mistake. I know I have to make them to learn from them and we all grow from our experiences. I've understood my mistake and I will do everything to make sure it doesn't happen again.'

After the excuses came the chatting. About everything and more. Paul talked about Juve, where, unlike at United, he said he felt appreciated: 'The players believe in me, the manager believes in me, I have the opportunity to play.' Among his teammates, Buffon and Marchisio were the ones who surprised him most and then there was Pirlo 'impressive, incredible, it's amazing to play alongside him.' What about Conte? 'He's more serious than Ferguson in training. He requires maximum focus. I like him because he's a winner. All he wants to do is win and he makes you understand how. I think I can improve a lot with someone like him.' He explained that he wanted to improve his box-to-box play: 'I have to be good at defending but also at attacking. I have to get better at picking up the ball and being more careful about how I deal with it and where I send it. I have the legs to defend as well as to attack, and I have to work on this quality.' As this was the first interview he had given in Italy and because the fans had not yet got to know him, the two editors of the Turin daily asked him to talk a little about himself. 'I'm a normal guy. I like listening to music, talking to my brothers on the phone, staying at home with my family, playing video games and going shopping. What do I spend the most on? Clothes. I got this from my mother. Sometimes I change twice a day. Fashion is my little weakness.'

What were the interviewers' impressions? That he was a determined guy with his head on his shoulders. That he could become the new idol of the *bianconeri*. What was certain was that Paul Pogba would give it his all. On 19 January 2013, under a grey Torinese sky that threatened snow but in the end was just cold, the *bianconeri* were playing the blue shirts of Udinese at the Juventus Stadium. It was the 41st minute and the score was stuck at 0–0. The young French player, sporting a yellow Mohican, took a seemingly innocuous ball out of the air outside the area, 35 yards from the opposition's goal. What did he do? He fired a curving shot violently with the outside of his right foot. Some claimed it even came close to reaching 100 kilometres per hour! Padelli, the Udinese goal keeper, could do nothing. The meteorite grazed the crossbar and hit the back of the net. A flash of lightening, a masterpiece, pure class. In the second half he even scored again. In the same style. A similar missile but this time along the ground. In the 66th minute, Paul was under pressure from Allan when he got away with a roulette almost worthy of Zidane, loaded his right foot and shot into the right corner. It was the birth of PogBOOM! Pogba's booming shots were something he had learned in England, where there is no time to lose taking the ball to the goal, so they shoot from anywhere on the pitch because sooner or later it's bound to go in. A catapult from distance was to become Pogba's trademark. Whenever he got anywhere near the outside of the box, the packed J-Stadium would shout: 'Shoot, shoot, shoooooot!!!' This honour was reserved for the French player. Paul talks about it in a fun video released by Juventus in which he explains how he kicks these screamers. At the end, he turns to the viewers and says: 'If you keep on shouting shoot, I'll keep on doing PogBOOM!'

It had not taken Paul many games to become an idol. The kids loved his Mohican, his hair graffiti, his style and his dance steps, even if he had yet to discover the Dab. Pogba, now twenty, took the loss to Bayern Munich very badly indeed. It ended 2–0 to the Bavarians in Germany, a result that was repeated in Turin. The Germans went through to the semi-final and the *bianconeri* said goodbye to Europe. Luckily, the talented player won his first *scudetto* with Juventus on 5 May with a 1–0 victory in Palermo. The second of the Conte era. The 29th in Juve's history. It was a shame he also received his first Italian red card against the Sicilian team. He spat at Salvatore Aronica, the Palermo defender, who clouted him in the face in return. A three match ban. A lesson to be learned at the end of a magnificent season. He finished it with 37 appearances (league and cup) and five goals (he had scored another of his bombs at Siena in the league on 24 February). He was a revelation to everyone, the surprise of the Serie A season.

Chapter 15

Light Blue and Dark Blue

The team sheet was released on 23 May. Twenty-one players were picked to take part in the Under-20 World Cup to be played in Turkey from 21 June to 13 July 2013. Paul Pogba was on the list. He was even named as one of the squad's leaders, alongside the Real Madrid central defender Raphaël Varane. It was an event eagerly awaited by the generation born in 1993. An event that Paul Pogba had nevertheless come close to missing.

The manager at that time, Pierre Mankowski – who has since left the role but remained at the FFF as an observer – clearly remembers the days before the announcement of his squad for the competition. 'Yes, at one point, I thought I was going to have to do without Paul Pogba. He was my captain but there was also a doubt hanging over his participation. There was a difference of opinion at the federation. Should he be picked or not? It was a little tense, I can tell you,' he admits from his Paris home.

Why was the situation so unclear? Simply because, during the 2012–13 season, Paul had seen the doors to the France senior team open to him and his first steps had been eventful to say the least. In early March, Didier Deschamps had chosen to take a closer look at what the player could do. The Bleus manager firstly took the time to talk to Pierre Mankowski, explaining to his faithful lieutenant that joining the first team would not necessarily call into question

Pogba's presence with the Under-20 team at the World Cup in Turkey. He also contacted his friend and Juve manager, Antonio Conte, who confirmed his thoughts about the French player over the phone. 'I told Didier Deschamps that he wasn't a player for the future but a player for the present, and that he should give him his chance,' confessed the former Italian international at the time.

Deschamps called upon Juventus's young hopeful for two qualifying matches for the 2014 Brazil World Cup that were to be played four days apart at the Stade de France against Georgia and Spain. 'I have other players in the midfield but they don't have the same profile, particularly in terms of attacking efficiency,' explained the French manager when he announced the squad for these two highly anticipated matches to the press. 'I want to see Paul with us, to see him live and train with the squad. He's a player for the future and the future is being built today.'

The announcement from Deschamps came on 14 March, the day before Pogba's twentieth birthday. It was a wonderful birthday present for *La Pioche* and it resulted in a first selection in the starting eleven on Saturday 22 March at Saint-Denis, in front of many members of his family. In a light blue shirt, Paul played for the full 90 minutes in the 3–1 win over Georgia that allowed the French team to top Group I ahead of Spain after four games played. However, the present that had seemed so wonderful at first glance, soon turned sour the following Tuesday against the Roja, then both world and European champions. On the pitch at Saint-Denis, the teammates of Sergio Ramos, Gerard Piqué and David Villa helped open the scoring in the 58th minute with a goal from Pedro, who got past Patrice Evra before beating Hugo Lloris. In the middle of the pitch, Paul did not let his head drop and worked hard to reduce spaces and disrupt the Spaniards' short, sharp passing game as best he could. He did everything within his power to stop his opposite numbers Xavi, Iniesta and Xabi Alonso. Whenever he could he also put pressure on the keeper Victor Valdes. As always, he refused to give in. From the touchline or on the pitch, his teammates were impressed by his work rate and maturity. Paul was determined to make his mark, unfortunately too determined ... In the 77th minute, in a fiercely contested aerial battle with Xabi Alonso, he received a warning for a knee in the back of the future Bayern Munich player. Just one minute later, the France team's number 19 was given a second yellow card, this time for showing his studs in a late tackle on Xavi. He had got carried away, allowing his will to win to turn into anger before it exploded. In the stands, his friends and family were dismayed. Paul applauded Viktor Kassai's decision. A way of challenging and containing his frustration. He turned his back on the Hungarian referee and went back to the Stade de France dressing room with his head hanging. While winning only his second cap, Paul had found a way to show what he could do but this was not quite how he had imagined it. No French international player had ever been sent off in their second only match. He was making his mark on the history of the Bleus in a very sad fashion.

In the post-match press conference, the kid from Roissy-en-Brie tried to ease his disappointment by talking to journalists about his premature exit: 'When I was sent off I hardly touched Xavi. But as the Spanish knew I was already on a yellow card that wasn't deserved they made the most of it. He touched my foot, fell over and started screaming. That's football. Of course, I'm mad at myself for causing trouble for my team'. A few minutes earlier, in the dressing room, he apologised to his teammates, promising to learn his lesson.

The 1–0 defeat jeopardised the France team's chances of topping Group I and qualifying directly for the 2014 World Cup. The other bad news of the evening came from Pogba's sending off, which placed a question mark over his continued selection for the Bleus. The Turin player would not be able to serve his suspension for France's first team before the next qualifying match on 6 September 2013 in Georgia. In the meantime, Deschamps' team was scheduled to tour South America to prepare, with two gala matches against Uruguay and Brazil. At the same time, Paul was also in demand for the France Under-20 team, which was preparing to play in the famous World Cup in Turkey for its age category.

'We asked ourselves a lot of questions,' admits Pierre Mankowski. 'We didn't really know if we could play him in the Under-20s after the red card he'd received with the first team. Eventually, once we got the green light from the international bodies, Didier Deschamps decided to allow us to use him. I remember Paul joined up with the squad very late. He arrived with a big smile on his face. He was delighted to be back among his friends. He was already our captain before he went to play with the first team, and although he now had a different status, he remained the same and was fully committed throughout the competition.'

For this final Under-20 phase, France were drawn in Group A alongside the United States, Ghana and Spain. This did not prevent the Bleuets from starting out with big ambitions given that the top two teams in each group would qualify for the quarter-finals, as would the two best third-placed teams. 'Even if our squad was up-and-coming, we were aiming for the title,' remembers the central defender Naby Sarr, who has spent time at both Sporting Lisbon and Charlton Athletic. 'We wanted to do great things in Turkey and Paul's presence was obviously reassuring. He had experience at the highest level after a great season with Juventus and two appearances for the France A team. That gave him a particular status but he was not the only one in the 1993 generation, far from it.'

There were in fact a lot of good players who are now with some of Europe's biggest clubs in the squad: the goalkeeper Alphonse Areola (PSG); the defenders Raphaël Varane (Real Madrid), Lucas Digne (FC Barcelona), Samuel Umtiti (FC Barcelona and Kurt Zouma (Chelsea FC, on loan to Stoke City); the midfielders Charles Kondogbia (Inter Milan) and Mario Lemina (Juventus); and the strikers Yaya Sanogo (Arsenal, now at Toulouse), Jean-Christophe Bahebeck (PSG) and Florian Thauvin (Olympique de Marseille). It was a boon for the coach Pierre Mankowski, who went on to say: 'I was lucky to have at my disposal players who were both great footballers and true teammates. They had been living together for five years, and the leaders they had at the beginning were still there. Paul was one of those, as was his roommate Geoffrey Kondogbia, as well as Raphaël Varane, Samuel Umtiti and Yaya Sanogo. He was very popular off the pitch. He took an interest in others and that was reflected in the general atmosphere They were a tight-knit group, united and perhaps also out for revenge after two semi-final defeats in the Under-17 and Under-19 Euros.'

France started the competition on 21 June against Ghana, recent runners-up in the Africa Cup of Nations. There was not much fun to be had thanks to the stifling heat when the World Cup kicked off on the pitch at the Ali Sam Yen Arena in Istanbul. At what had been the home of Galatasaray, Paul Pogba's teammates took nearly an hour to get the measure of their opponents. Having scored in mid-June during the two last warm-up matches against Greece and Colombia, the France captain this time left it up to Kondogbia, Sanogo and Bahebeck to find the back of the net in the 3–1 win. Nor would he take the penalty during the second match three days later against the United States. Yaya Sanogo scored his second goal in the competition but it was not enough to prevent France conceding a 1–1 draw and finding themselves in danger for the third and final group match against the Spanish team of Jesé (PSG, on loan to Stoke City), Saúl Ñíguez (Atlético Madrid) and Paco Alcácer (FC Barcelona). 'We weren't in a good place before that match,' confirms Naby Sarr. 'Especially because Paul was suspended.' The French captain had managed to collect two cautions against Ghana and the United States that kept him out of the decisive game against the Spanish generation that had been crowned Under-19 champions of Europe a year earlier. 'Although our squad had plenty of depth, it was obviously a big loss,' continues the manager Pierre Mankowski. 'But despite his disappointment at not being on the pitch, he played his role as captain all the same.' I remember that at half time, he spoke to the group and said they couldn't possibly leave it at that. That the guys needed to react. In the end, we lost 2–1 but his intervention resonated throughout the competition.'

Despite this defeat against their bogey team of Spain, France benefited from Ghana's decisive 4–1 win over the United States and finished second in Group A. The Bleuets had got into the last sixteen through the back door. 'The defeat against Spain may have been a blessing in disguise. It really stung,' admits Naby Sarr. 'We found ourselves with our backs against the wall when it came to playing the host nation in the last sixteen.'

On 2 July, the small Kamil Ocak stadium in Gaziantep was jumping. The 15,000 seats quickly found takers for this blockbuster game between Turkey and France. In the town close to the Syrian border, there was plenty of support for the young national team, as much as if it had been a match disputed by the local Gaziantepspor club. 'This match was one of the turning points in our competition,' confessed Mankowski. 'In an incredible atmosphere, we played a great match and won 4–1. We didn't give them any chances to believe and that gave us incredible strength for the rest of the competition.' The return of Paul Pogba to the midfield was no coincidence when it came to the new side shown by the young French players.

'He was all over the midfield. He picked up countless balls,' remembers Sarr. 'He also brightened up our game, like the second goal when he put Lucas (Digne) through perfectly for Jean-Christophe (Bahebeck) to finish. From then on he was unstoppable.'

In the quarter-final, Pogba scored his first goal of the tournament from the penalty spot following a foul on Bahebeck. He comfortably wrong-footed Amanov, the Uzbekistan goal keeper, in the 4–0 win. In the semi-finals, the number 6 did not score but stood firm and imposed himself on the midfield during the rematch against Ghana (2–1). Two goals from Florian Thauvin sent France into the Under-20 World Cup final for the first time in its history: 'Two years earlier, the 1991 generation of Griezmann and Lacazette had reached the semi-final. We had already done better than they did but we didn't want to stop there. They had made their ambitions clear before the tournament and wanted to achieve their objective,' said Jean-Paul Delayes, one of the staff members.

On 13 July 2013, Pierre Mankowski's France returned to the Ali Sami Yen Stadium in Istanbul, where they had begun the competition three weeks earlier. Uruguay, who had beaten Nigeria in the last sixteen (2–1), Spain in the quarter-final (1–0 after extra time) and a surprising Iraq team on penalties in the semi-final (1–1, 7–6), would take on the Bleuets. Despite the stakes, Paul was not overawed at all; on the contrary, he used the pressure to produce football of the highest level. 'He was everywhere against Uruguay,' remembers Naby Sarr, who lined up in the central defence alongside Kurt Zouma in the final. 'He showed that he was already a great player. He swept up the ball and gave it back to you cleanly every time. He was also very active offensively. He was the nerve centre of our team.' Pierre Mankowski confirms: 'He was everywhere and it wasn't surprising. That was his character. As long as I've known him, he has wanted to be the best midfielder, the best defender, the best striker and, if he could, the best goalkeeper. That's Paul Pogba.'

No goals were scored during the 90 minutes or during extra time. The title of world champion would be decided by penalties. 'Obviously he wasn't going to chicken out. We had to find five penalty takers. He put himself forward and even asked to take the first one.' In his dark blue shirt, Paul Pogba faced up to the Uruguayan keeper to set an example for his teammates and show them the way forward. He tried to expel the pressure by looking up high into the Turkish sky. This allowed him to forget the whistles that surrounded him as he placed the ball on the spot. He started slowly before sprinting up. A diagonal shot that grazed the post. Goal! Paul did not waver and, just as he had done against Uzbekistan, he had wrong-footed the best goalkeeper in the competition, Guillermo De Amores. He could breathe again, even taunting the Istanbul public, who were siding with the Uruguayans. Now it was up to his teammates to play, the French goalkeeper in particular. Alphonse Areola was inspired. He blocked two of the first three Uruguayan attempts. From a distance, Paul encouraged the fourth French spot kicker, Dimitri Foulquier. The right back, who had trained at Stade Rennais but been with the Spanish team Granada since 2013, managed to score despite a piece of inspiration from the Uruguayan goalkeeper. The French team won 4–1, taking the crown from the Brazilian team of Danilo (Real Madrid), Oscar (formerly of Chelsea) and Philippe Coutinho (Liverpool), who had won the title two years earlier in Colombia.

In the warm Istanbul night, the young Bleuets raised the Under-20 World Cup. As always, Paul, the captain, was at the centre of things. It was he who lifted the precious trophy. He also had his own personal award: Pogba had been voted the player of the tournament ahead of the Uruguayan Nicolás López and the Ghanaian Clifford Abogye: 'There are no words for how I'm feeling. I'm happy and proud,' he explained after the match, holding his trophies. 'It's something exceptional. A dream come true. We've made our mark on history. Future generations will talk about us.'

Paul left his captain's armband in the dressing room before boarding the bus back to the team hotel. He had become one of the lads again, a mood-maker and joker par excellence. He went from seat to seat in fits of laughter, stirring up the crowd: 'So, guys. Are we world champions or not? Who did you say were the world champions?' The players started chanting again: 'France!'

'We spent all night celebrating that title,' recalls Naby Sarr. 'French football hadn't won a World Cup since 1998. Paul had lit the touch paper. He's the same on and off the pitch. Someone who shares their joy.' He likes to joke around and dance. He just loves life!'

Chapter 16

Golden Boy

At the entrance to the Turin editorial offices of *Tuttosport* a gold panel hangs above the sofa in the waiting area. You cannot help but look at it. The first two lines, in tiny characters, record that the European Golden Boy award was founded by *Tuttosport* in the autumn of 2003 and is awarded every year to a footballer under the age of 21 playing in a European nation's top tier. The third line, in bold capitals, reads: 'The 2013 winner is the Juventus player Paul Pogba, who literally decimated the competition.'

On 4 December 2013, the sports daily dedicated its front page to Paul, with a huge colour photo, announcing that the young French player had been voted the best young footballer of the year by an international jury of thirty sports journalists. He beat Romelu Lukaku, Julian Draxler and Raphaël Varane, the twenty-year-old Frenchman. Pogba succeeded Isco, the 2012 winner, on a golden roster packed with illustrious names: Wayne Rooney (2004), Lionel Messi (2005), Cesc Fàbregas (2006), Kun Agüero (2007) and Mario Gözte (2011). He was the first Juventus player to win the junior Ballon d'Or and, like those who had preceded him (e.g. Messi), he also dreamt of winning the grown-up version. He talked about it, without false modesty, on 4 December at Saint Vincent in the Aosta Valley at a gala event. Looking extremely dashing in a tuxedo, white shirt with a bow tie and gold Mohican, the young French player held up the prize with a smile on his face. He granted press and TV interview requests willingly.

'How does it feel to be considered the best young Under-21 player in Europe?' they asked him. 'I'm happy and proud,' he said with confidence.

'When I think back to when I was a child and I wanted to do this job, I wanted to win a prize like this. Now my next objective is to win the other golden ball.'

The Juventus midfielder recalled that in 2012 he was on the shortlist of fifty, but was 'still young and hadn't played enough to be able to aspire to winning the title. I supported the Belgian, Thibaud Courtois, the Atlético Madrid goalkeeper. He came third, I think. I'm flattered because this is an important recognition that has marked the career of some phenomenal players.'

Who was he dedicating the trophy to? Obviously to his family: 'To my mother, Yeo Moriba, to my dad, Fassou Antoine, to my big brothers, Florentin and Mathias. And also to my teammates here at Juve, to the club, to my fans and of course to my agent, Mino Raiola.' Raiola had compared him to a Claude Monet painting. Pogba laughed and said: 'Mino is crazy!'

Among the dedications and memories, Paul reflected on the year that was drawing to a close and what was yet to come. '2013 really has been a golden year for me,' said the twenty year old from Roissy-en-Brie.

It was impossible to claim otherwise. Thanks to his talent and character he had won over his team, manager and fans; he had become PogBoom, made his debut for the French national team, won the *scudetto* and conquered the Under-20 World Cup with the Bleuets. And it was certainly not going to end there: the 2013–14 season had got off to a great start.

18 August 2013, Stadio Olimpico, Rome, the Italian

Super Cup, Juventus v Lazio. The 21st minute of the first half: Claudio Marchisio, who had sustained a knee injury in a clash with Radu, could not continue. Conte sent Paul on. After two minutes, Andrea Pirlo took a free-kick on the edge of the penalty area. Rather than shoot he tried a routine practised in training and kept the ball short to Lichtsteiner on the right. The Swiss player pulled it back into the box and the ball rebounded off Radu but then fell at Pogba's feet; Paul turned and, with a powerful left-footed shot, found the angle needed to pierce Marchetti's goal. Juve 1 Lazio 0. After the break, the *bianconeri* ran away with it (4–0 was the final result), but it was the French player who had changed the face of the game. He had unlocked the match and provided Carlos Tévez, the Argentine apache who had just arrived from Manchester City, with the final goal of the game. The Super Cup showed Juventus in impressive form and saw them stake their claim to yet another *scudetto*. For Paul it was a second title with the *bianconeri* and he was also delighted to have been picked as man of the match. It was a shame the boy's happiness had to be ruined by racist chanting. In the Curva Nord of the Stadio Olimpico fans had ululated at Pogba, Ogbonna and Asamoah, Juve's three black players. Every time they touched the ball racist boos rained down on them. The shame of Italy Sir Alex Ferguson had told the young French player about had become a reality. Paul was furious. He told *France Presse*: 'They're ignorant. I was alone out there against 30,000. Those people behave in that way even though they have black players in their team: it's a real lack of respect, also to the players who wear their team's shirt. It's an unpleasant situation but I'll keep playing and stay focused on my job.'

For once, the racist boos did not go unpunished. Lazio would play their first league game against Udinese without spectators in the Curva Nord.

The 112th Italian football league season began on 24 August 2013. Antonio Conte admitted that Pogba was 'growing, it will be hard to keep him on the bench.' He had climbed the ladder and was no longer just a powerful midfielder with pace but now had the numbers to be a starting eleven player in his own right, as well as Pirlo's deputy. When the *bianconero* veteran was not available it was up to the twenty-year-old French player to orchestrate the Old Lady's midfield. Paul was rarely on the bench. He almost always played and put on a show, just as he did in the Turin derby on 29 September. He took it upon himself to do away with Torino: in the ninth minute of the second half, the French player scored after Tévez hit the crossbar. The controversy as to whether Tévez was offside exploded, but Juve won the derby – at the expense of Torino, who had not beaten the *bianconeri* in eighteen years – and knocked Napoli off the top of the table. It was the sixth match of the season and a first league goal for the Juventus number 6. In November, Pogba's goal tally rose to four. He scored against Fiorentina and Parma and, on 7 November at the Juventus Stadium, killed off the big match against Napoli (3–0). His goal was stunning: he picked up the ball on the edge of the penalty area and, with a fierce right-footed shot, beat Pepe Reina with a torpedo he never even saw coming. Paul had got a taste for booming shots from a distance as well as for inflicting misery on the poor Neapolitans. Given the results of his first year at Juventus, it was clear that on 4 December Paul Labile Pogba would be crowned the best Under-21 player in Europe by the media. And given his success in 2013, it was also clear that they would ask him what he wanted to win in 2014. He replied: 'Well, you'd like to win everything but then your opponents get in the way! And whenever they're playing Juventus, they're always up for a fight. But if dreaming is allowed, in my dreams I would love to win the league, the Champions League and the World Cup with France. With my feet on the ground, I would say that a third Italian title in a row with Juventus would be a historic achievement.'

Dreaming was allowed but, as he said, reality meant dealing with opponents. The first dream to vanish was the Champions League. Juventus failed to get out of the group stage. They finished behind Real Madrid and Galatasaray in Group B. The defeat (1–0) on 10 December under the Istanbul snow proved to be fatal. They could console themselves with a third place finish that meant the knock-out phase of the UEFA Cup. The first leg was in Turin, on 20 February 2014, against the Turkish team Trabzonspor. Pogba scored his first goal in European competition. It came in the 94th minute. Tévez provided the assist to the French player, who sent the ball squarely into the Turkish net. It was his seventh goal across league and cup competitions. Those worth remembering included one against Atalanta on 22 December, exactly half way through the season, and, in particular, another PogBoom against Sampdoria on 18 January 2014. The boy with the Mohican was just outside the area, studied the situation carefully, looked to see where the Sampdoria keeper was, controlled the ball and then, with his right foot, unleashed one of his slingshots from 25 yards out. It ended up in the far top corner. Da Costa could do nothing. Paul ran off and lifted up his black and white striped shirt to reveal a white t-shirt printed with RLS CITY BOYS. This was the name Paul and his friends had given themselves when they were kids at La Renardière. Paul had not forgotten them. He paid tribute to them by pointing at the writing and proudly reminding them that even if so many things had changed for him, where he came from had not. He had grown up, both as a man and as a player. Antonio Conte, now the Chelsea manager, had been able to help him in this evolution, although perhaps it would be more apt to call it an explosion. In just a season and a half, Conte had instilled in him, through long conversations and the odd scolding, three golden rules: work, commitment and focus. But above all he had tried to clean up Paul's youthful vices. These included unnecessary dribbling in front of the defence, backheels in midfield and flashy play, in short putting on a show for the sake of it. Conte had tried to get the French player to play in the most simple, most straightforward way possible. He gave him the efficiency required in a midfielder. Paul had listened to Conte's long-winded speeches and lectures and had put his advice into practice. Just as he had listened to the suggestions of Fernando Llorente, the Spanish striker, his friend and roommate for away matches. Paul had stolen ground from Claudio Marchisio and become, with the freshness and brazenness of his almost 21 years, a linchpin in the *bianconero* midfield. He had also seen his name at the top of the shopping lists of major European clubs. The pretenders included Paris Saint-Germain, Carlo Ancelotti's Real Madrid and Pep Guardiola's Bayern Munich. Beppe Marotta had to clarify that he would not be selling any of his big players in the January transfer window, nor was he considering doing so in the summer. For the boy from La Renardière, there was talk of a possible contract renewal and a salary increase. But it would take time for Mino Raiola and the Juventus directors to come to an agreement.

Another dream died for the Golden Boy on 1 May 2014. This time under violent rain at the Juventus Stadium, when the *bianconeri* could only manage a 0–0 draw in the second leg of their UEFA Cup semi-final against Benfica. The Portuguese had won 2–1 in the first leg at the Estadio da Luz. They closed the door on the match in Turin. Juventus fought valiantly but there was nothing they could do. Europe remained a mirage. The final, which would coincidentally be played at the J-Stadium, would see the Portuguese face off against the Spanish team Sevilla.

The domestic league could be counted on to raise *bianconero* morale, as ever. Three days after the European debacle and, on 4 May, Roma were unexpectedly taken apart at home by Catania (1–4), making Juventus champions. For the third successive time. One of Paul's dreams had come true. The Old Lady had not managed such a feat since the 1932–33 season. In the three remaining matches, the team from the capital sank further while Juventus continued their triumphal march. They finished the season with 102 points, a record, putting seventeen points between themselves and Roma. They had won 33 matches of 38 played. They also had the best attack and the best defence in Serie A (80 goals scored and only 27 conceded). The Golden Boy had the highest number of appearances (36 in the league, 51 in total) and had scored nine goals across all competitions. Pogba explained to *L'Équipe*: 'This year will stay in my memory because it was hard, long and required so many sacrifices. Playing every three days, as well as the sacrifices, also requires taking responsibility: you can't do what you want to do, you have to train, play, rest, train, play, rest. You learn and grow professionally. You go out less, you spend less time with your friends, you've got to eat well, to rest and recover quickly. I went through a tough time, I started to feel tired, and I wasn't at my best. But I had to deal with it, manage it and keep going. I had to react because great things were expected of me. The Brazil World Cup with France was just around the corner.'

Chapter 17

To Brazil, alongside Messi and Neuer

In the early summer of 2014, Paul's galaxy changed once and for all and there was no doubt he realised it. An evening in Roissy-en-Brie was all it took for him to understand that he had taken on a new dimension. On 7 July, almost a thousand people turned out to greet him at the town's reception hall: friends, former teammates and even anonymous fans who had waited for several hours to applaud French football's new star. The eyes of the local kids were sparkling. One, who was braver than the others, even shouted out to the Juventus midfielder before he turned his back on the crowd and was swallowed up by his friends and family: 'Paul, we're proud that you've come here to see us,' yelled the kid, who must have been about twelve years old and was sporting a France shirt. 'We're all behind you. You've given us something to dream about.' Paul Pogba savoured these encouraging words as a broad smile broke out across his face. Three days earlier, the France team had been beaten in the quarter-final of the World Cup at the Maracanã Stadium in Rio de Janeiro.

The 2013–14 season had seen Paul Pogba's international career take off. After his sending off in his second match against Spain, he was not about to miss out on his third chance. This came with another qualifying match for the Brazil World Cup, played on 10 September 2013 at the

Gomel Central Stadium in Belarus. Against a solid team led by the former Barcelona and Arsenal player, Alexander Hleb, *La Pioche* nonetheless took more than 45 minutes to get going. At half time, while Deschamps' players were behind against all expectations, Patrice Evra had no hesitation in shaking up his former Manchester United teammate. It should be said that Paul was clearly at fault for the first goal scored by Egor Filipenko after half an hour of play. He was caught out like a beginner in the air and the big striker from FC BATE Borisov took advantage of the opportunity to score his first headed goal for the team. 'They've no right to move us around like that,' could be heard in the narrow corridor that led the players back to the dressing room. But fortunately, Paul made up for it in the second half. The French broke down Belarus and imposed themselves 4–2 with a final goal scored by Pogba. On the end of a cross from Mathieu Valbuena that was mishandled by the home team's defence, he wrestled free to push the ball into the back of the net and open his account with the France team in his third match. Although not everything had been perfect, far from it, Paul had scored points. 'It's clear that he has an impressively strong character for his age,' noted Dimitri Payet after the win. Mathieu Valbuena was also impressed by his new teammate's work rate: 'It's a delight to play with him. He reads the game well and comes forward. He has a lot of potential.'

The following matches confirmed this trend. Alongside PSG's Blaise Matuidi, the Turin-based player became Deschamps' first choice in midfield. In October, he was in the starting eleven for a friendly against Australia at the Parc des Princes in Paris (6–0), then played for the entirety of the final qualifying match, won 3–0 against Finland at the Stade de France. Paul was also a key cog in the *Tricolore* machine during the play-off game against the Ukraine, one of the team's last chances to get to Brazil. On 13 November in Kiev, Laurent Koscielny (Arsenal) was the best French player on the pitch during the first half. Despite the collective failure after half time – two Ukrainian goals scored by Zozulia and Yarmolenko – Paul kept his head high and never gave up. Four days later, for the return leg, he was once again in the 4–3–3 that was made for him. Alongside Matuidi and the Newcastle United playmaker, Yohan Cabaye, he made sure he was the boss. Paul kept everyone entertained by alternating his long and short game. Although he failed to score any goals, he again scored points. France overturned the deficit against the Ukraine by winning 3–0 with two goals from the Liverpool central defender, Mamadou Sakho and a third from the Real Madrid striker, Karim Benzema. The result sent the French to Brazil and guaranteed – at least that was what people were already imagining – a leading role for Paul Pogba at the 2014 World Cup.

When the France team arrived in Brazil on 10 June, Pogba had become the Bleus' main attraction. The absence of Bayern Munich's injured star, Franck Ribéry, gave him greater exposure, as did his second Italian league title with the *bianconeri*. There was plenty of eagerness to see Paul Pogba at work in Brazil. 'When the French players arrived in the country, he was the most applauded player,' noted the Brazilian daily sport newspaper *Lance!* 'This is a further sign of his responsibility in the team. He also seems to have the confidence and mentality required to take on this role.' It was true that in the meantime Paul had taken advantage of the warm-up matches that followed qualification against the Ukraine to get a little more comfortable in the heart of the French team. He won four more caps between March and June 2014 and scored his second goal for the team on the end of a cross from Mathieu Valbuena; a headed goal, it was the first of four French goals against Norway on 27 May at the Stade de France.

In the aftermath, he loudly proclaimed his ambitions to the journalists with whom he was popular: 'I'm happy and proud of myself. I'm starting to make my dreams come true. But that's not it, now I have to play well and win. I hope with all my heart that we can do it.'

Paul had found his niche with the Bleus. He felt at home both at the Clairefontaine château and the Ribeirão Preto base where the French were staying during the tournament. In 'Uncle' Pat (his nickname for Patrice Evra), he had found a formidable intermediary to introduce him to the older players. He often shared a room with the Real Madrid defender, Raphaël Varane, also part of the Under-20 World Cup-winning team. He also already had a very friendly relationship with Antoine Griezmann (Real Sociedad), who had joined the France team at the beginning of the year. Pogba was comfortable but was he too comfortable in Deschamps' eyes? At that time, the French manager had spoken to the media several times to try to calm his protégé's enthusiasm. After his goal against Norway, he warned: 'It all seems very easy for him but he mustn't end up feeling too at ease because in the end that can be counter-productive. At the highest level it's about maximum focus. He's going to have to fight that a bit. He has to block out everything superfluous that doesn't bring anything important either to him or to the team.'

Didier Deschamps was also worried about the excitement around the 21-year-old phenomenon: 'He's still a young player when it comes to the highest level. He has a media circus around him and a look that seems to be very important. What interests me is obviously what he does on the pitch. But inevitably what happens off the pitch can disturb his head a little and that should not be allowed to take precedence.'

The start of Paul Pogba's World Cup was encouraging nonetheless. On 15 June, at the Beira-Rio stadium in Porto Alegre, he celebrated his first appearance in the competition against Honduras by winning a penalty in the 45th minute that led to Karim Benzema opening the scoring just before the break. While he was waiting to receive the ball from Cabaye, he was shoved in the back by Wilson Palacios, who collected his second yellow card in the process and was sent off as a result. In the first half, the two players had already clashed and Paul had narrowly missed being sent off himself by trying to take the law into his own hands.

After coming off with an hour gone during the opening 3–0 win, Paul was a substitute five days later in Salvador de Bahia against Switzerland (5–2). This did not prevent him from making his mark with an assist, shortly after coming on for Karim Benzema in the 67th minute.

Despite this, his record was tarnished by his third Group E match against Ecuador. On 25 June at the Maracanã in Rio de Janeiro, the Bleus disappointed with a lacklustre 0–0 draw against the South American team. Paul was not saved this time by Deschamps, who left him on the pitch until the very end. The comments were unforgiving: adjectives such as 'irritating' and 'self-satisfied' came thick and fast to those charged with writing detailed accounts of the match. Paul had done a Pogba. He had provided a glimpse of his talent but overplayed to the point of gifting Ecuador with a goal scoring opportunity in the second half. Although he hit the post at the end of the match it was not enough to extinguish the fanned flames of a fire or the flood of critics who claimed that his level of play was far from what it had been for Juventus and that he was too nervous, not playing with the right rhythm and guilty of too many technical errors. The fears voiced by Didier Deschamps before the competition had resurfaced. It was Jean-Michel Larqué – a former French international with AS Saint-Étienne and PSG in the 1970s who has become an influential pundit in France over the past two decades – who was responsible for reigniting the debate. Over the *RMC* airwaves, he not only called into question Pogba's performance against Ecuador but also his behaviour in general: 'Even if I'm not with the France team day in day out, I feel that Paul Pogba's attitude means "I'm just as good as the more experienced players." There are things that are not popular with Didier Deschamps as a manager. Paul Pogba's concern at the moment should be keeping his place. He does not behave like a player of his age towards his elders.'

Paul Pogba was on the front line before the decisive last sixteen game that saw France take on Nigeria, runners-up in Group F behind Argentina and ahead of Bosnia and Herzegovina, and Iran. Before the knockout game, the French closed ranks and publicly supported the young midfielder. Yohan Cabaye spoke up: 'As far as I'm concerned, he has had some good games. He's an important player in our team. After that, I don't know what you're expecting of him, to score two goals or dribble the entire length of the pitch?' His manager went on: 'I don't know everything that's been said or written. The most important thing to me is what I have to tell him. He needs to be encouraged. He does not need to have his faults pointed out, but what he does do well should be praised because he does plenty of good things.'

And to support his comments, the manager who had launched him into the first team and made him his control tower in the midfield, reiterated his confidence in the player by once again picking him in the starting eleven on 30 June at the Estadio Nacional. This time Paul was up to the task. And in style! While France were struggling in the first half against Nigeria, he held firm in the midfield, sweeping up balls and hardly letting anything go. In the 22nd minute, he unleashed a splendid volley that forced the Super Eagles' keeper, Vincent Enyeama, into an equally masterful save. This was the real Paul Pogba, never as strong as when he is cut to the quick with his back to the wall. In the second half, at the height of battle, he took on the guise of national hero by breaking the deadlock in the 79th minute: he took advantage of a corner from Mathieu Valbuena that had been badly cleared by Enyeama to head the ball victoriously into the open goal. 1–0. While you might imagine an exuberant celebration, this time he kept his joy inside, almost silently. He allowed himself to be surrounded by his teammates but showed no reaction. It was as if he did not want to show his anger after the wave of criticism that had broken over him. Paul Pogba had silenced his detractors; that was the most important thing, especially as he sent the Bleus into the quarter-final of the World Cup.

Of course, in private, he reverted to his natural state. Back with his Bleus teammates, *La Pioche* put on a show. During the dinner that followed the 2–0 win over Nigeria – the second goal was a Yobo own goal – he became the entertainer amusing his teammates with an improvised dance. The response to his performance against Nigeria on social media was unanimous. In the space of just a few days, his followers had risen by nearly 500 per cent to almost 800,000 fans. Pogba mania would not subside, even though he was powerless to stop a German 1–0 victory in the quarter-final on 4 July. Paul went down fighting at Rio's Maracanã. The best French player in the first half, he was one of the few to compete with the world champions in waiting and fought throughout the 90 minutes. Only the final whistle could quash his hopes of a World Cup-winners medal. He could console himself with the title of the tournament's best young player, ahead of his friend Raphaël Varane and the Dutch player from PSV Eindhoven, Memphis Depay, part of the team eliminated on penalties by Argentina in the semi-final. An award in this competition saw him join the ranks of some of the greatest players: Messi (Golden Ball for the best player), Manuel Neuer (Golden Glove for the best goal-keeper) and James Rodriguez (Golden Boot for the top goal scorer). It was not a bad way to mark time while waiting for better things to come.

Chapter 18

Road to Berlin

He wipes his tears with his shirt and walks towards the bench. Once there the pitiless TV cameras zoom in on him, crying as he covers his face with his hands and dark-coloured anorak. On 18 March 2015, a magical night in Dortmund that saw Juventus admitted to the last eight of European football, for Pogba there was only bitterness and anger. His match against Borussia would last only 26 minutes. A clash with Sokratis Papastathopoulos, the BVB 09 Greek defender, left him on the ground clutching his right thigh. The medical staff could do nothing but accompany the player off the pitch. It was true that two days before the match, alarm bells had begun to sound when the number 6 had pulled up in training, but it had seemed nothing more than a knock when instead it was in fact very serious. Paul limped to the team bus after the game. The *bianconeri* were decidedly concerned. There was already talk that the French midfielder would miss the Serie A game against Genoa, would not be able to respond to Didier Deschamps' international call-up and would be out for both legs of the Champions League quarter-final. Tests the following day revealed the worst: a second-degree lesion of the myotendinous junction of the right biceps femoris muscle. Two months out. His season was practically over. Pogba would only be able to return if they made the Champions League and Coppa Italia finals, while he would probably only be able to play in the final two league games against Napoli and Verona. It was bad news for the talented French player and a serious loss for Juve at a decisive stage in the 2014–15 campaign.

It was a season that had begun for Paul with one shock and two wonderful surprises. First came the shock. Antonio Conte, the manager who had taken Juve to the *scudetto* for three years in a row, left. On 15 July 2014, he said goodbye to the *Vecchia Signora* following differences of opinion over the transfer market and a decline in motivation. A month later he became the manager of the Italian national team, taking the Azzurri to Euro 2016 in France. His place on the Juve bench was taken by Massimo Allegri, the former AC Milan manager. Fans of the *bianconeri* were not happy with the choice, and criticism of the Livorno-born 46-year-old Tuscan came from all sides. They would be forced to change their minds.

Then came the surprises. On coming back from his holiday in the US, he found an old friend at Vinovo: Uncle Pat. Evra, his father figure, the defender who had helped him find his feet, both in the French national team and in Manchester. Evra had left the Red Devils for Juventus. It was great news for the boy from Roissy-en-Brie. And that was not all: on 4 August, his brother Mathias also moved to Italy, from Crewe Alexandra to Pescara. From Cheshire to Abruzzo, from Football League Two to Italy's Serie B. Paul was happy for Mathias. Pescara is only a six-hour drive from Turin.

If the summer had brought interesting changes, the autumn put an end to the saga of his contract renewal. Beppe Marotta, the CEO, chose the Juventus shareholders' meeting on 24 October 2014 to officially confirm the French player's signature. Paul's marriage to the Turin club would last until 2019. The Golden Boy would see his salary triple.

If the numbers in the contract signed in 2012, due to expire in 2016, provided for a salary of €1.5 million per season, this had now increased to €4.5 million. Having witnessed that summer's attention from Chelsea, Paris Saint-Germain and Manchester United, Juve had to loosen their purse strings whether they wanted to or not. Pogba was happy. He immortalised the moment of the signing with a post on Twitter and thanked the club and its fans 'for their support.'

Eight days after the tweet, Paul found a way to really show his gratitude. On 4 November, Juventus were playing in the Champions League against Olympiacos at the J-Stadium. It was the fourth game in Group A, but two defeats (against Atlético Madrid and away against the Greeks in Athens) had left the *bianconeri* needing a win at all costs. It was raining cats and dogs and things took a turn for the worst when, in the sixteenth minute of the second half, N'Dinga scored to make it 2–1 to the Athenians. Juve reacted and Llorente, who had just come on in place of a listless Morata, equalised thanks to a deflection off Roberto, the Greek keeper. Another twist favoured Pogba. He received the ball inside the box with his back to goal; he tried an impossible backheel to supply Carlos Tévez, but the ball fell back at his feet for him to turn, shoot and slot it into the left hand corner of Roberto's net. 3–2 to Juventus. They had qualified for the last sixteen of the Champions League.

Juve's first knockout tie would be against Borussia. The first leg in Turin on 24 February ended 2–1 to Juve. The second leg in Dortmund on 18 March finished 3–0 to Juventus, including a headed goal from Pogba. Until that night in Germany he was stringing together performance after performance. He was significantly improving his record as a professional. One goal in the Champions League, against Olympiacos, one in the Coppa Italia in the 6–1 win inflicted on Verona on 15 January 2015, and six league goals. Some were impressive, including the one that opened the scoring at the Stadio San Paolo in Naples on 11 January. It was a great goal. Paul the Octopus picked up a loose ball in the Neapolitan area and volleyed it to the left of Rafael. It was a goal that paved the way for the eventual 3–1 win, revenge for the Italian Super Cup was served. It avenged the defeat of three weeks earlier when the Neapolitans had won 6–5 on penalties in Doha (2–2 after extra time) and taken the trophy home. Not only that but the *bianconeri* had broken a curse. It had been fourteen years since they had last won at the San Paolo. They also extinguished Napoli's hopes of getting back into the *scudetto* race. Paul Pogba would score his last league goal before his injury against Sassuolo on 9 March in the 26th league game of the season. It was another of his gems. At a pace, or better, at a gallop, he tamed a difficult ball and tried a shot without even thinking about it and it really came off. With power and precision, there was no question of the ball not ending up in the back of the net. The French player ran with his hands up to his ears to listen to the roar of the J-Stadium. It was the 82nd minute and the winning goal that saw Juventus move eleven points clear of second-placed Roma. The *scudetto* was within reach. In the mixed zone Paul smiled with his eyes and in flawless Italian said: 'It's true, it was a great goal. I'm happy, but the most important thing is the win. We've taken a big step forward in the league but we have to remain 1000 per cent focused.'

It was a shame that he would have to watch the title-winning game from the stands. It was 7.46pm on 2 May 2015 when Paolo Valeri blew the final whistle for the end of the match between Sampdoria and Juventus at the Luigi Ferraris stadium in Genoa. With a single goal from Arturo Vidal, the *bianconeri* won 1–0. Four games before the end of the season, they had secured the 31st league title in their history, the fourth in a row and their first under Allegri. The manager, in whom few had had faith, was thrown in the air by his players and managerial staff on the Genoese pitch. It was party time in the stadium and in the dressing room, as well as in Turin. Intense but not excessive; three days later Real Madrid would be paying a visit to the Juventus Stadium. It was the first leg of the Champions League semi-final. Another match that Pogba would miss, just as he had missed the quarter-final against Monaco. Alvaro Morata and Carlos Tévez would keep the dream alive against the defending champions. The Spaniard got on the scoreboard in the eighth minute; Cristiano Ronaldo evened things up in the 27th and the Argentine finished things off from the penalty spot in the 58th. Eight days later, the French player was present for the return game in Madrid. Massimiliano Allegri had given him a run out in the league against Cagliari at home on 9 May. After being out for 52 days, he showed he was not yet match fit. He played 63 minutes before being substituted by De Ceglie but scored the goal that temporarily gave Juve the lead: a shot from the edge of the area from a corner that Ceppatelli deflected to wrong-foot his keeper.

'I ran and didn't feel any problems. We're on the right track,' he said hopefully after the game. 'He had a good comeback,' added his manager. 'He trained with the team for two days. We now have three more days to prepare for the game and we hope everyone will be in good shape.'

13 May 2015, 8.40pm. Wearing blue, Paul Pogba passed under the blue UEFA arch heralding the Road to Berlin. He was there, at the Bernabéu against the *Blancos* of Cristiano Ronaldo and Carlo Ancelotti. In the first twenty minutes, Bale, Benzema and Ronaldo all tried their best from all over the pitch in all sorts of ways, but Juve held firm, gritting

their teeth. Then Chiellini took James down in the box and the Swedish referee, Jonas Eriksson, blew for a penalty. Gigi Buffon failed to pull off a miracle when faced with Cristiano Ronaldo's crisp right-footed shot down the middle. In vain, he had gone to the right. 1–0 to Madrid. The Bernabéu roared. The *Merengues* persisted and besieged Buffon, who began to lose it with his defenders. But then came the former Madrid player – the boy who had grown up at the Casa Blanca would get his revenge, demonstrating his worth to the fans of his former club and silencing the 60,000-strong crowd. He scored the goal that saw Juventus qualify. A free-kick by Pirlo from the right, a tangle in the box and a punch from Casillas that cleared the ball. Vidal tried to put it back in; Pogba grazed it with his head and Morata came in like a train, controlled it with his chest and unleashed a left-footed shot. The shot bounced off the turf, flew away and ended up in the back of the net. Goal: 1–1. The *bianconeri* still had another 27 minutes to suffer but in the end it was Juventus who would make the trip to Berlin and to the Champions League final, twelve years after losing to Ancelotti's AC Milan on penalties in Manchester.

It was pure joy on the pitch at the Bernabéu and in the dressing room. Of course, it would not be easy in Berlin against none other than the Barcelona of Messi, Neymar and Suárez, but many were starting to believe in this team. Their appointment at the Olympiastadion was set for 6 June. Before that, Juve would win the double. After a wait of twenty years, they won the Coppa Italia. At the Stadio Olimpico in Rome, Allegri's team beat Lazio 2–1 after 120 minutes. The *bianconeri* fans were already dreaming about the treble, something that had only happened once in Italy, with José Mourinho's Inter in the 2009–10 season. They dreamt of being able to lift the large-handled cup after nineteen long years. It felt like an age since 22 May 1996, when Juventus had beaten the Dutch team Ajax on penalties.

Paul Pogba, just 22 years old, had the chance to play a leading role in the final. Although he had only scored one goal in the Champions League and had missed a number of matches due to injury, this was his breakthrough season, the season of his maturity, of full international recognition. It was undoubtedly also the high point of his years in black and white. He had played very well in 2015, even if after the game against Verona, the last of the league season, he had been scolded by Allegri for 'too much showboating.' A few days later, Paul responded to his manager's criticism in a long interview with *La Stampa*: 'I don't do it on purpose, but sometimes it seems as if I relax a bit. I repeat, this is me, it's my personality and I don't do it on purpose. I play my football, I play my game. It's how I am, it's not arrogance. How did I take Allegri's scolding? As a piece of advice: I have to be focused throughout the entire game, I always have to give my best.' After promising to be on his best behaviour, Paul talked about his opponents and the final. 'Everyone knows how Barça play, they have the best attack in the world. You can train more tactically but this is not what will win you the game. We have to be aggressive and lucky. We know that we're not favourites but we will give it our all. It's a final, anything can happen. Messi is Messi, he's probably the best player in the world today in the best team in the world. Barcelona are very good, but we're in the final and we have nothing to lose. I like their game, I like watching them play. But I would like to see them lose on 6 June.'

A question: 'Would the final be Paul Pogba's last game in a black and white striped shirt?' The boy gave a confident response: 'I've never said that and people can believe whatever they want to.' That was as maybe, what was certain was that Paul was the most sought-after midfielder in Europe. His name was on everyone's lips. Starting with Mino Raiola, his agent, who indulged himself in artistic comparisons; Paul was a Monet, a Van Gogh, a Basquiat who had a value on the transfer market of €100 million, €120 million, €130 million because, the Dutch-Italian agent explained: 'The transfer market is a sport in its own right that runs parallel to football. And the value of a player does not depend on the club selling him but the club buying him.' On paper at least, there were plenty of clubs prepared to take part in an auction for the talented French player. Every month, or almost every week, another potential buyer came forward. There was Paris Saint-Germain, who enquired about prices and costs, but apparently did not get as far as making a concrete offer. There was Manchester City, who, according to the English tabloids, were prepared to put €100 million on the table, not to mention that the player's salary would be somewhere in the region of €14 million. And it did not end there: back in England there was interest from Chelsea and the Special One in person, who had made his intentions clear a year earlier. Florentino Pérez's Real Madrid were also in the running. They initially denied making an offer but then sent in none other than Zinédine Zidane on a reconnaissance mission. 'Pogba is fantastic,' he told *RTL*. 'And what I like about him is that he has everything: he's a complete player. He knows how to score because he's good coming forward. In terms of his footballing skill he's really extraordinary. It's obvious that top clubs like footballers with his kind of talent. He can grow and improve and he needs a healthy environment around him.' At Real, of course.

Barcelona were also jostling for pole position in the race for Pogba. Josep Maria Barthomeu and Johan Laporta, candidates for the presidency of the Catalan club, had made the French player an electoral promise during their campaigns. Apparently, thanks to the sporting director at Barça and Barthomeu's envoy, Ariedo Braida – a former director at AC Milan and best man at Marotta's wedding – the deal could be done for around €80 million. The agreement with Juve was close to being signed, or at least that was what they were saying in Barcelona. The *blaugrana* had first refusal. 'If Juve wanted to sell Pogba, we would have been the first to make an offer,' Albert Soler, director of institutional relations at Barcelona, would say some time later. 'But in the end Juve decided not to sell him, to wait for a year, and we didn't need to buy him.' However, for Pogba and the Old Lady it would be a long summer of transfer rumours. Even after Berlin. What happened in the final is well known. With goals from Ivan Rakitić, Luis Suárez and Neymar, Barça won their fifth Champions League and reproduced the treble of the Guardiola era. Juve lost their sixth final in eight attempts. Many blamed the penalty that never was, when Dani Alves held Pogba back inside the box. Also because, after the break, Barcelona struck on the counterattack with Suárez, who was quick to pick up a short parry from Buffon following a shot from Messi. 2–1 and, as Juve were trying to pull off the impossible, another counterattack came from Neymar to finish off the game. When it was over, Paul Pogba went to console Morata, who had scored the goal that had momentarily drawn Juve level. A few days later, the French player confessed to the microphones of *Canal+*: 'After pulling it back to a draw we were convinced we could go on to win. It hurts to lose. There was also a foul on me that should have been a penalty, but the referee didn't see it. But it was my first final. Congratulations to Barcelona, who deserved to lift the cup. I learned a lot from this game, I saw the cup and I hope to be able to lift it one day.'

Chapter 19

The Number 10

It is just a number. But it weighs heavy on your back. It means a lot. Because it is magical, because it is sacred, because it is a symbol, because it points you out to the world, because it earns you respect, because you always have to live up to it. Because you can play without a number 9, as Spain did in the 2010 World Cup in South Africa, but without a number 10 no football of any kind can withstand an onslaught. Because the number 10 is fantasy, poetry, philosophy, heart and head. Because the number 10 is the artist, the raw talent, the director, the conductor, the motivator, the best. Because the great empires of football have been built on the number 10. One of the greatest national teams of all time was forged around Pelé's number 10. The hand of God appeared with Maradona's number 10. The face of the devil revealed itself on the football pitch through Zidane's number 10.

Whenever you mention the number 10, nostalgia comes to the fore and a longing for a time in football when a coach would tell his team to 'watch out for the number 10.' When there was less muscle and more grey matter. When football was an entirely different thing to what we see now. Mention the number 10 and you'll find yourself faced with list upon list of the best number 10s in history. Pelé or Maradona, Puskás or Hagi, Messi or Francescoli, Zico or Zidane, Platini or Baggio. Mention the number 10 and everyone has their favourite, depending on their country, club and age. Every team has their altar of number 10s, past and present. Juventus's is well-stocked. From King Platini to Luis del Sol, from Liam Brady to Fabio Capello, from Omar Sívori to Roberto Baggio, ending up with Alessandro del Piero and Carlos Tévez. The Apache was the latest to wear the shirt with the double figure. But after two seasons in black and white, 50 goals, two league titles, one Coppa Italia and one Super Cup, he said a fond farewell to Juve on 13 July 2015 to return to the team closest to his heart: Boca Juniors. The number 10 was without an owner. Who should it be given to? The club thought it over and made their decision on 6 August. It was to be Paul Pogba's turn. The choice was dictated more by marketing and reasons of image than anything else. Paul the Octopus was an unusual number 10: he was not the classic entertainer, the captain or the team motivator. But he was very popular among the younger generation. He had the most long-term marketing potential, could sell the most shirts and could replace Alex 'Pinturicchio' del Piero in the collective imagination of the *bianconeri*. In spite of the rumours of a departure at the end of the season that became more and more pressing.

On finding out about his new number the man in question tweeted: 'It's an honour for me to wear the Juventus number 10.' Massimiliano Allegri said that 'Paul asked for the number 10; he will have more responsibility because it isn't easy to wear that number: it's been worn by some of Juve's greatest players.'

It is hard to say whether or not it really was the Frenchman who asked for it. It seems doubtful in terms of how tough he would find wearing it and given that he seemed to prefer the number 6. Whatever the case, it was his for the time being.

His first match with the number 10 on his back took place on Saturday 8 August at the Shanghai Stadium. It was a success: Juve beat Lazio to win the Italian Super Cup. Two new signings gave the Turin team their first title of the season: Mario Mandžukić, the Croat, who had arrived from Atlético Madrid, and Paulo Dybala, the twenty-year-old Argentine bought from Palermo for €32 million. The two strikers were not the only new players in Allegri's team. The club on Corso Galileo Ferraris had decided, after winning four league titles, that it was time to bring in some new blood: Sami Khedira, Juan Quadrado, Alex Sandro, Daniele Rugani and Simone Zaza. In addition to Tévez, other departures included Pirlo, who was bound for New York, Fernando Llorente, who was returning to Spain, Sevilla to be precise, and Arturo Vidal, who had accepted an offer from Bayern Munich.

It was a very different Juve that greeted Paul on his return. A Juventus without his friend Llorente, missing Vidal and with no sign of Pirlo. The maestro who had taught him to read the game, to be decisive, to be calm and have faith in himself, to be serene on the pitch and who triggered his lightning runs with millimetre-accurate passing. It is also worth adding that things were not the same with Allegri as they had been with Conte. His relationship was different, very different, to how it had been with the manager from Lecce. It was true that after training the Tuscan would take him to one side and challenge him to mini-goals or baskets, taking shot after shot to see who would be the first to make it to fifteen as Dybala watched on. But Allegri was not the confidant and storyteller that Conte had been. Not someone who would spell out to Paul, over and over again, what he wanted from him. Allegri would shout at him whenever he showboated or lost the ball unnecessarily. In short it was a changed Juve, he had a different relationship with his manager, was wearing the number 10 on his back, and had to take Pirlo's place in driving the *bianconero* midfield forwards. It was not easy. 'I have more responsibility in this Juve,' Paul explained in an interview with *La Repubblica*. 'I had Pirlo alongside me before and one of the opponents was always on him. Now they put them on me.' 'Did he feel like a number 10 now?' asked Emanuele Gamba, the journalist. 'What does that mean? I'm not a number 10 in terms of my position on the pitch. I feel like a midfielder and it's an honour to wear the number of those who've won the Ballon d'Or. It's an important shirt in the history of Juventus and I want to do it proud. But when I look at my shirt I don't see my name or the number, I only see Juve and I want to give 100 per cent. And win.'

Winning, a word that Juve struggled to pronounce in the autumn of 2015. They lost their first two league games, at home against Udinese and at the Olimpico against Roma. The champions of Italy and Champions League runners-up flopped. Zero points, something the *bianconeri* had not had at this stage since 1912–13! They did not get their first win until the fourth game of the season, away from home against Genoa on 20 September: 2–0, with a Pogba penalty in the 60th minute. But it was a flash in the pan. Juve were not clicking. Either because Allegri needed to rejig his formations; or because some key figures had left; or because the new arrivals had yet to find their feet; or because injuries were seeing the *bianconeri* take a beating from all sides. On 28 October, a 1–0 loss to Sassuolo sent Allegri & Co. properly into crisis. It was their fourth league defeat and it left them languishing at eleventh in the table, eleven points off the top spot. Many thought Juve were done for. They would need a miracle to get back on track and back into the title race, the papers said. Gianluigi Buffon angrily told the TV cameras: 'We were unworthy, undignified. At 38 years old I don't want to look like I don't know what I'm doing. We're a great team and we shouldn't allow something like this to happen.' It was an appeal to the leaders of the team, to get them to roll up their sleeves, win back the dressing room and steady the ship. And that was exactly what happened. But the trial had already begun. The manager, the style of play and the new strike force were all in the dock, but the harshest criticism was reserved for Paul Pogba.

Fans, directors and pundits were all asking what had happened to the number 10, the player who had wanted to be a new type of midfielder. Someone who did everything: defend, attack, score, win tackles and provide assists. A mixture of Vieira, Deschamps, Zidane, Ronaldinho, Henry, Ronaldo and Messi. What had happened to the footballer with so much class? Where was the champion, the golden boy with the talent everyone craved? Where had the €100-million man disappeared to? He was nowhere to be seen on the pitch, he was like a ghost, a missing pawn on the black and white chessboard; the ball was not at his feet as it should be, nor was he the leader he was supposed to and wanted to be. What had happened to him? The number 10 shirt was weighing him down more than it appeared. He felt the responsibility and was trying too hard, striving to win every game on his own: in the end it all went wrong. It seemed the number really did not work for him. So much so that on 25 October, Paul turned up on the pitch for a league game against Atalanta with a '+5' written on his back in felt tip pen. Some thought it was a tribute to Pelé, who had turned 75 two days earlier. It was not a tribute though but something Alberto Ferrarini, a motivator and numerologist from Cornuda in the province of Treviso, had come up with. Ferrarini had begun working with Leonardo Bonucci some time ago while he was at Treviso, when the centre back, who would eventually line up for the national team, was more often on the bench or in the stands for the Serie B team than on the pitch. Ferrarini had been helping Bonucci for years as he moved from Treviso to Juve, then into the national team. His methods have become the stuff of urban legend. The story goes that before an important game he once locked Bonucci in a dark basement and asked him to scream out all his anger, and that he would give him garlic-flavoured sweets to motivate him, telling him that they were what Roman legionaries used to eat before going into battle. Whatever the case, what is certain is that Bonucci introduced the motivator to Pogba. Ferrarini, who has also worked with cyclists such as Alessandro Ballan and Marco Bandiera, loves numbers. Let's take a closer look: '1+0+5' makes '6', the number the French player had worn until the previous season, the shirt with which he had won three league titles with Juventus and the Under-20 World Cup with France. The number 6 was good. There was more: '1' and '5' together are '15', the French player's birthday.

What is not in doubt is that Pogba used a marker pen to add a number 5 to the back of his shirt. When asked to explain it, he was vague: 'Yes, maybe I did do it to make my old number 6, but sometimes I do things like that with my hair because I feel like it.'

Whatever the explanation, the boy got over the block caused by the number 10 or the €100 price tag that had been put on him and went back to playing as he knew best. He scored on Halloween, when the kids in the Juventus Stadium came in fancy dress holding up 'trick or treat' signs. He scored the opening goal in the Turin derby. A pass from Quadrado, a feint from Dybala and Paul the Octopus unleashed one of his bullets from the edge of the area. It flew under the crossbar and into the back of the net. Bonucci was one of the first to hug him after the goal and a delighted Paul mimed the '+' and the '5'. The game finished 2–0 and marked the turning point for the *bianconeri*. From 31 October 2015 they went on a streak of 25 fantastic results (24 wins and a single defeat). A miracle that led to a dream comeback. By December things were already looking decidedly better. Juve qualified for the last sixteen of the Champions League from a group that pitched them against Sevilla, Manchester City and Borussia Mönchengladbach. They were just three points off the top of the table before the Christmas break. Back in the race for the *scudetto*.

Paul, the boy who had been taught while in Turin to rest in order to play his best, to work hard, to eat well, to eat pasta, pasta and more pasta, was smiling again. Just as he was on 20 December 2015, when he unveiled his Dab to the world. Juve were 2–1 up away at Carpi thanks to two goals from Mandžukić. Just as the second half was getting under way, Marchisio launched a long ball, an assist for Pogba who, finding himself alone in the Carpi box, controlled the ball with his chest and foresaw that Belec, the Carpi keeper, would come off his line. Goal! He ran to the touchline, dropped his head, stuck out an arm and folded the other one to his chest. It was pure geometry. What kind of a way was that to celebrate a goal? In time everyone would discover the Dab dance and its origins. That it came into being on the hip hop scene in Atlanta everyone was in agreement, as they were on the roots of the term: dabbing, in the United States, means to consume cannabis oil. On where the dance came from, however, no one could agree. Some said it had been invented by singers on the Quality Control Music label. Others talked about Migos, a rap trio that popularised the movement with the Bitch Dab. Others insisted that it had been started by Skippa da Flippa, Peewee Longway, Jose

Guapo or Soulja Boy. What was certain was that it crossed from the world of hip hop to the NFL and the NBA. Cam Newton, the Carolina Panthers' quarterback, performed it at every game. An example that would be followed by basketball players, such as LeBron James, the Cleveland Cavaliers wing, and D'Angelo Russell from the Los Angeles Lakers. Even Hillary Clinton performed it on TV with Ellen DeGeneres during the US presidential campaign.

It is a short hop from the US to Europe, and Paul, who loves everything American and the NBA in particular, imported the celebration. He performed it with his new partner in crime Paulo Dybala and involved the Juventus dressing room and directors. Even Pavel Nedved thought nothing of lowering his head and bending his arm. Pogba was not the only footballer to indulge in the Dab: Mario Balotelli, Jesse Lingard and Romelu Lukaku, among others, followed suit. But Paul even managed to convince Andrea Agnelli, the president of Juve, and tough guy Edgar Davids to dab. For an Instagram post. It happened in Zurich on 11 January 2016, the night of the *France Football* and FIFA Ballon d'Or gala. The young French player was in attendance with his mother, Yeo. He turned up with a two-tone Mohican (gold and black), glasses, bow tie, white shirt and a black suit embroidered with a gold floral motif. Whether it was trashy or fashionable will be for posterity to judge. It was certainly a look that got him noticed among the eleven FIFA FIFPro World XI. The Juve number 10 had been selected by the jury to be part of the team of the year. He smiled on stage for a family photo alongside Marcelo, Thiago Silva, Sergio Ramos, Dani Alves, Andrés Iniesta, Luca Modrić, Cristiano Ronaldo, Messi and Neymar. Speaking of photos, or of selfies, Paul did not miss the opportunity to immortalise the moment with the three 2015 Ballon d'Or candidates. He had

made the shortlist of 23 but was not among the three final-
ists: Cristiano Ronaldo, Lionel Messi and Neymar. For the
fifth time the award went to Messi, who, standing alongside
Pogba, lived up to his nickname: *La Pulce* (The Flea).

'I hope to win the Ballon d'Or myself one day but there's
a lot of work to do. I have to keep going as I have been.
Today is an important victory if I think about where I started
out. I'm happy for myself but I want even more for all those
who've helped me get onto this stage,' said the Frenchman,
who once again played down rumours of his departure. 'Yes,
I did sign a Barcelona shirt but that doesn't mean anything.'

Chapter 20
For Sale

16 March 2016, 8.45pm. Juventus were preparing to play a key match in the knockout stages of the Champions League against Bayern. Paul had missed the first leg on 23 February in Italy; it had ended in a draw (2–2). His motivation for the return match was high. His first coach, Sambou Tati, as well as several of his friends from La Renardière were in the stands. They had arrived in Bavaria the day before and gone straight to the Charles Hotel in Munich to help him celebrate his 23rd birthday. They had given him a black and pink US Roissy shirt. Disappointing them on match day was out of the question, all the more so because, as the two teams came out onto the pitch in Munich's Allianz Arena, the eyes of the 70,000 spectators were trained on him, or rather, on his feet. For the first time, the Juve midfielder was sporting black and gold boots made by Adidas. Running down each heel of these high-backed boots, christened the 'Ace 16+ Purecontrol', were the words 'POGBOOM' and 'POGBANCE' in large letters. The insole read 'I Am Here to Create'.

Adidas had picked their moment well, taking advantage of this clash between two heavyweights of European football to announce the new partnership through a well-crafted marketing campaign launched only a few hours before the kick-off: 'This is the first sponsorship contract I have signed and it was a very important decision for me. I chose Adidas because we are united by our passions and values. We have the same style on and off the pitch. Adidas share my dream for a new creative and modern football. I hope to be able to leave my mark and bring something stimulating and new to this iconic brand. The best is yet to come. This is Pogboom! I love music, dance and fashion but my greatest passion is football. I need a brand that gives me the space I need to express myself and explore new frontiers. With Adidas, I've found a partner that shares my objectives,' *La Pioche* explained in the press release.

The duration and worth of the agreement were not disclosed. According to the Italian media, notably *La Gazzetta dello Sport*, the partnership was said to rest on a €4 million annual deal for a period of ten years, in other words a total of €40 million over the duration of the contract. The French international was joining the Adidas team, which already featured some huge stars, such as the Barcelona players Lionel Messi and Luis Suarez, Gareth Bale of Real Madrid and the Gunner, Mesut Özil.

Adidas were, of course, delighted: 'This is a big coup for us because he plays for a superclub. Euro 2016 is also on the horizon and Paul is expected to be one of the key players in the France team. We're counting on a ten to fifteen year partnership. Having Paul with you is a bit like buying your dream house,' said a delighted Benoît Menard, Adidas's director in Paris, in the documentary '*La folie Pogba*'. In the same programme broadcast on *L'Équipe 21* in May 2016, experts called upon to provide their opinion on this marriage with the German brand were to some extent divided: there were those, such as Nouredine El Haoussine (Sports Universal Music and Brands), who were already comparing the Juventus player to a 'rock star like Neymar, more edgy than Eden Hazard and with more star quality than Messi,' and others such as Sébastien Bellerecontre (4success), who thought it was a sensational move: 'Given that the player has a showman side and comes across in a relaxed and playful way.' However, this opinion was not shared by Gilles Dumas, a communications expert with Sportlab: 'We all agree that Pogba has value. But this sum just seems amazing to me today. Adidas are taking a gamble. They're gambling that Pogba will have become the first or second best player in the world in five years' time. Basically, they're looking for a replacement for Ronaldo and Messi, and Adidas think it might be Pogba.'

The cleverly orchestrated marketing coup became a stroke of genius in the sixth minute of the game against Bayern Munich. Put through by Khedira, the Swiss right-back, Stephan Lichtsteiner stumbled in the German box. The ball fell at the feet of Paul Pogba, who struck a right-footed shot between the legs of the defender Joshua Kimmich and into the bottom of the net deserted by Manuel Neuer. His first Champions League goal of the season. Paul had held his nerve, and, although there were still 80 minutes left to play, as things stood, Juve had qualified for the quarter-finals of the competition.

The match was far from over but by now Paul was used to fighting. To secure his golden contract with Adidas, he had had to spend the last few months embroiled in a tough behind-the-scenes battle with his former adviser, Oualid Tanazefti: 'Since November 2014, the player was no longer the owner of his image as he had entrusted the entire "Paul Pogba" brand to Tanazefti and his associate Ylli Kullashi.' explained an insider, who prefers to remain anonymous, like most people given to comment on this subject.

The secrets of the contract ceding image rights were revealed by Mediapart in December 2016, based on

documents produced by Football Leaks: for a sum of between
€1.8 million and €5 million, Paul Pogba is said to have
allowed the Luxembourg company 'Koyot Group', owned
by Tanazefti and Kullashi, to recover 30 per cent of the
profits on the signing of a new contract, while the two men
were already receiving a salary for their work. Paul Pogba
would keep 70 per cent of the profits but could not touch
the money until 31 October 2029. He would only receive
an annual fee of €33,000. Conversely, his representatives
would have their hands free for fifteen years to invest the
player's fees wherever they wished without justification and
recovering half of the profits. Still according to Mediapart,
Paul would have to pay back the sum invested at the beginning (between €1.8 million and €5 million) in 2029, while
Tanazefti and Kullashi would retain the right to re-sell this
image contract without his agreement.

The French insider continues: 'When Tanazefti fell out
with the Pogba family and found himself isolated, the image
rights contract was all he had left. It was a shame for the kid,
who ended up stuck. It was also a way for Tanazefti to have a
return on his investment, given that he had been with Paul
Pogba since almost the very beginning.'

It was only a month later, in December 2014, when Mino
Raiola learned of the affair. 'He asked his lawyers to do everything within their power to break the contract and even
appealed to the legal departments of some major brands,'
continues the insider, who specialises in talented young players. 'But it was rock solid and unassailable. He then asked
Paul to try to negotiate directly with his former mentor to
attempt to find an amicable way to recover his image rights.
Tanazefti, who did not want to do Raiola any favours, had
begun offering the contract to Chinese investors and the
Doyen Sports company, and even to Jorge Mendes, Cristiano

Ronaldo's agent. But he did not find any takers because Raiola carries a lot of weight in that world and no one was interested in putting his back up.'

After the Pogba camp threatened to bring the matter before the courts, negotiations eventually resumed between the two parties. Tanazefti is said to have initially demanded €15 million but received a third less. An agreement was finally reached in early 2016: for a fee of €10 million (€6 million for Tanazefti and €4 million for Kullashi, according to Mediapart), Raiola bought back the image rights of his player. According to the Football Leaks documents, the Dutch-Italian agent is believed to have founded a company in Jersey to manage the 'Paul Pogba' brand and it is understood that it was the directors of this company who signed the contract with Adidas. 'This affair has become a case study in football,' says a French sports adviser. 'It shows young people the dangers of this type of contract. A person's rights over their image is a fundamental notion in French law and the athlete must not under any circumstances transfer these rights to a third party.'

Things were also getting tougher on the pitch in Munich. Paul was everywhere. As Juventus were 2–0 up thanks to the Colombian Juan Cuadrado, Pogba was showering gifts on his strikers: after picking up a spilled pass, he crossed from the left to provide Cuadrado with the chance to score a second goal just before the break, but Neuer had intervened. Nor had Paul forgotten the Spaniard Alvaro Morata, supplying him with two clear opportunities, but both times the Real Madrid player had missed the goal and the opportunity to kill off the match.

Instead of leading 3–0, Massimiliano Allegri's team now found themselves with the tricky possibility of extra time. Thanks to Robert Lewandowski in the 73rd minute and

Thomas Müller in injury time, Bayern had wrestled back a 2–2 draw that meant parity across both legs. Despite what may well have been one of his busiest matches of the Champions League season, Paul was powerless in the 108th and 110th minutes: buoyed by their fans, the German champions, who had thought they were out of the competition, pulled away with goals from the Spaniard Thiago Alcantara and the Frenchman Kingsley Coman. As if to sum it up, as Bayern's fourth goal was being scored by his compatriot, Pogba was brought down by Kimmich. His objective of a second Champions League final was in tatters and his thoughts about leaving at the end of the season may well have been confirmed on that sad evening in Bavaria.

'The night of 16 March 2016 was probably decisive for his future, said the French agent. 'On a footballing level, Paul realised that in order to continue growing and to win the Champions League and the Ballon d'Or one day, he would have to go somewhere else, to a more competitive league, such as in Spain or England. For Mino Raiola it was time to take action because the profile of his player thanks to the Adidas contract and the recovery of his image rights in particular opened important doors to him when it came to negotiating a future transfer.'

Even better news for the Dutch-Italian agent was that *La Pioche* went out with a bang during the final games of the Italian season. These performances were punctuated at almost every match by complaints from the *bianconeri* fans: '*Non si vende, non si vende* [Not for sale! Not for sale!]'. On 20 March, he scored a free-kick in the derby against Torino, which Juve won 4–0; in April, he scored two goals from corners, one a match-winner in the 2–1 victory over AC Milan at the San Siro and the other during a 4–0 stroll against Palermo at home. When he was not scoring himself he was showing what his teammates could do with no fewer than seven assists in the last nine Serie A games: three for Mandžukić, two for Morata and two others for Sami Khedira and Simone Zaza.

If Europe was still a bit too big for him this season, he was clearly starting to feel cramped in Italy. In 2016, he was undefeated in Serie A (he was suspended for the only loss against Hellas Verona in the 37th match) and strung together an incredible series of 26 undefeated league games, including 25 victories, between 31 October 2015 and 14 May 2016. Juventus secured their 32nd *scudetto* ahead of Napoli and Roma by nine and eleven points respectively. Paul finished his fourth season top of the class with eight goals in Serie A (ten across all competitions) and provided the most assists in the league (thirteen), tied with his future replacement at Juve, the Bosnian Miralem Pjanić, then at Roma. As everything continued to go right for him, on 21 May 2016, the *bianconeri* won the Coppa Italia to secure another double. In front of more than 67,000 spectators at the Stadio Olimpico in Rome, the Turin team needed almost the full extra time period to wait until the 110th minute for Alvaro Morata to get the better of Riccardo Montolivo's Milan. At just 23 years of age, Paul already had plenty of trophies under his belt: two Italian Super Cups, four Italian league titles and two Italian cups. His popularity was greater than ever after a fulfilling year on the footballing front. However, as the curtain came down on the 2015–16 season, Paul was experiencing his final moments in a black and white striped shirt: 'The Italian club had most likely already made up their minds to let him leave,' say the sports adviser. 'At that point there was a question mark over who he really belonged to. To Juve? Not really! To his future club? Not yet! Did he belong somewhere else then? Not sure!'

Chapter 21

From Dream to Disappointment

The tournament seemed to have been made for him. About that there was no doubt. He had come a long way since his stuttering start for the Bleus against Spain in 2013. Paul had grown up and surpassed the status of promising young hopeful that had been bestowed upon him two years earlier at the Brazil World Cup. His club experience, aura when playing for the national team and popularity among young people in particular made him one of the expected stars of Euro 2016.

In a France team that had won nothing since the Euro 2000 championship in the Netherlands and Belgium – which came thanks to a golden goal scored by David Trezeguet against Italy at the end of extra time – he would be show-cased in the same way as his teammate, the Atlético Madrid striker Antoine Griezmann. These two players were thought to embody the future as well as the present for Deschamps' team, which had lost several of its senior players along the way: Karim Benzema and Mathieu Valbuena were taken out of the running by the sex tape affair in October 2015 – the former was suspected of blackmailing the latter – while Raphaël Varane and Lassana Diarra were both ruled out injured at the last minute.

'We won't be able to say whether these Euros belonged

to the Pogba–Griezmann generation until they're over,' tempered the Juventus player while speaking to a journalist from *Le Monde* two days before the start of the competition. What he did know was that 'every time France play in a tournament at home, they win it. My aim is to win this one too. I'm prepared to do whatever it takes for the team. I hope the French fans will be there on 10 July. Even more than that. I want to make them jump with joy when I lift the cup!'

Paul is not the type to hide his ambitions and is not afraid to tempt fate. He already saw himself emulating the Bleus of Michel Platini's time, who had played uncomplicated French football and won the European Championship in 1984 with a 2–0 win over Spain in the final at the Parc des Princes, thanks to a goal from '*Platoche*' following a huge blunder from the Roja keeper, Luis Arconada. He also saw himself repeating the World Cup win of 1998, which had united the whole country behind its football team: 'I don't know if it has anything to do with the economy, but people were much happier in 1998 when France won the World Cup. A victory for the Bleus would definitely put a smile back on people's faces. I think it could have a big effect on the country.' Paul was five years old in 1998 but he remembered every detail of Christophe Dugarry's celebration against South Africa, Zinédine Zidane's red card against Saudi Arabia, Lilian Thuram's two goals against Croatia and the victory over Brazil in the final. More than anything, he remembered the crazy night of 12 July 1998, when he shared in the excitement with his two brothers in the small Roissy-en-Brie apartment, wide-eyed, counting Zizou's goals, chanting 'one, two, three, nil!', before going down into the street to celebrate the Bleus' success, yelling, jumping and even climbing on top of cars.

On 10 June 2016, it was his turn to line up on the pitch at the Stade de France in Saint-Denis, in Paris's northern suburbs. In its flagship stadium, France were getting ready to launch the competition with the opening match against Romania. The popularity of the team embodied by the faces of Pogba and Griezmann was immense. You only had to see the mass of blue shirts in the crowd bearing their numbers and printed with their names. You only had to listen to the ovation reserved for the two players when the team line-ups were announced over the loudspeaker: 'Number 15, Pauuuuuul …' and the fans chanted 'Pogba', echoing with some improvised Dabs here and there around the stadium. What if the dance became the hit of the summer?

The game was ready to start; France had not played a single competitive match since their World Cup quarter-final defeat against Germany in 2014. Qualifying automatically as the home nation, the team had only competed in warmup matches, of which Paul had played about fifteen, scoring two goals against Serbia and Portugal in the autumn of 2014. The French had been rubbing shoulders with some big fish – in particular, Germany, during the heart-breaking match of 13 November 2015, marked by a series of terrorist attacks around the Stade de France and across the city of Paris – but there is nothing like competition to judge the level of a team and to assess its ambitions in a tournament that, for the first time, brought together 24 nations. It went without saying that for both France and Paul Pogba, the three Group A matches against Romania, Albania (15 June) and Switzerland (19 June) would provide a better indication of what they could expect.

Paul played 77 minutes against Romania. He was the third and last of those who had started the match to give up his place, after Griezmann and Olivier Giroud. He was substituted for the last fifteen minutes by the young Manchester United striker, Anthony Martial. The home nation won 2–1 thanks to a lifeline of a goal from Dimitri Payet in the dying moments of the game. The verdict was harsh: 'Lack of precision,' 'lack of solidity,' 'lack of coherence.' To sum up, Paul's level was not in keeping with his new status.

Against Albania, five days later at the Stade Vélodrome in Marseille, both Pogba and Griezmann were on the bench. After half-time, he went on for Martial, who had seemed absent for most of the first half. As a result, *La Pioche* played a part in the French victory built on moments of inspiration from Griezmann and Payet. Although things had improved, he was still far from making an impression. The press latched onto 'lost balls and a misjudged challenge at the end of the match.' In short, bad choices and clumsiness.

Whatever the case, on 19 June, Paul returned to the starting eleven on the pitch at the Stade Pierre Mauroy in Lille for the final match against Switzerland that would decide who topped the group. He was one of the rare bright points in a disappointing match that ended 0–0. Playing on the left of midfield, this time Pogba lived up to his status with a solid defensive first half, providing the Bleus with some attacking strength thanks to three strikes, one of which hit the crossbar.

The performance went some way to boosting his mixed start to the competition and provided a glimpse of a possible increase in strength that continued to become clearer in the last sixteen against the Republic of Ireland. But when it came to making an initial assessment, it was his attitude that was troubling. Against Albania at the Stade

Vélodrome, Paul Pogba had celebrated his team's second goal in injury time in unusual fashion. After going over to congratulate Dimitri Payet, he made a rude gesture that some thought was directed at the press gallery. Paul's 'celebration' had gone almost unnoticed. And for good reason. At the request of the editorial director of *beIN Sports*, the sequence captured by an isolated camera was not broadcast on the channel. 'It was a personal decision for which I assume full responsibility,' said Florent Houzot, defending himself in the heat of the moment. 'We are all supporters of the France team and it was not the time to create a pointless controversy. *beIN Sports* is a premium channel that does not need to create a buzz to exist. I prefer to stay positive.' Controversy followed all the same. Photos were posted on social media before the Belgian TV channel *RTBF* broadcast the clip.

Paul's gesture inevitably recalled one made by his compatriot, Samir Nasri. After his equaliser against England during Euro 2012 in the Ukraine, the playmaker – who spent time at Olympique de Marseille, Arsenal, Manchester City and Sevilla – directed a 'sssh' gesture towards the press gallery, with his finger to his lips.

The affair had led to a media lynching of the player. At a home Euro, there was no question of reviving that scandal or further tarnishing the image of the French team, already well and truly damaged since the 2010 World Cup in South Africa.

Didier Deschamps quickly poured water on the fire saying he was satisfied with the explanation given by his player. Within 24 hours of the match, Paul Pogba sent a statement to the *Agence France Presse*:

'The joy I showed with some grand gestures, as I always tend to do, after Dimitri Payet's winning goal against Albania has now taken on controversial proportions after some found it to be rude.

I would like to say very sincerely but clearly that, whatever the interpretation given to these images, it was never my intention to make a point, to attack anyone or to exact revenge.

I was so delighted that the match ended this way and, as I turned towards the stand where I knew my mother and brothers were, I danced as I usually do and raised my arm and fist in the air.

Nothing more, nothing less.'

Paul did not say anything further on the subject He did not participate in any press briefings at Clairefontaine during the competition. Only his mother, Yeo Moriba, professed her sorrow at seeing her son accused in this way: 'Yes, I was a little annoyed that the gesture had been interpreted like that. But I know this gesture is a gesture of victory. My son has been brought up properly. Our response will come on the pitch.'

Unfortunately, the pitch did not do much to help. On 26 June, after just two minutes of play in the last sixteen at the Parc Olympique Lyonnais in Décines-Charpieu, Paul committed a foul on the Republic of Ireland striker, Shane Long, inside the box. The Southampton forward played it well and pushed the French midfielder too far. Penalty! Robbie Brady – formerly with Manchester United and now, at Norwich City – did not need to be asked twice to wrongfoot the French goalkeeper, Hugo Lloris, and give his team the lead.

Luckily for the French – as well as for Paul – a certain Antoine Griezmann decided to play one of the matches of his life. The darling of Atlético Madrid turned the match around by scoring two goals, one after the other, with an hour played. He flew to the rescue of his friend Paul Pogba, who would have been the perfect target if France had been eliminated. The joy of the two men was a pleasure to watch. Since the start of the competition, they had seemed inseparable and made their friendship clear in front of the French Football Federation camera. From keepie uppies in training that verged on circus tricks, to NBA PlayStation games and the odd impromptu rap, the duo seemed guaranteed to provide the atmosphere at Clairefontaine. 'We already knew that Paul was close to Patrice Evra, as they had both been at Manchester United and Juventus, but it was during this competition that we discovered his friendship with Griezmann,' noted Grégoire Margotton, a leading pundit for *TF1*. 'It would never really have crossed our minds before the tournament. Some people had reservations and were sceptical about the relationship, saying that their attraction came from their fame. For my part, I think it was sincere, I don't even dare imagine that it was just marketing.'

This friendship between the team's two stars was also clear to see on the pitch, especially during France's next two games. When they made short work of Iceland (5–2) in the quarter-final, Paul was completely transformed. He played with freedom, finally ruling the roost in midfield. His passing was good, his tackling unbeatable, his play simple and he scored for the first time in the competition. In the twentieth minute, the Juventus player jumped up into the Saint-Denis night to catapult a header inside the far post on the end of a corner delivered by none other than Griezmann. It was his first goal for France in more than a year and a half, dating back to 11 October 2014 against Portugal in the Stade de France. Just before the break, in the 45th minute, he also found himself on the end of a long ball before starting a move that, after a return pass from Giroud, put Grizou through to score.

The duo were up to their old tricks in the semi-final for the revenge match against the world champions. Germany lost 2–0 at the Stade Vélodrome in Marseille. Antoine Griezmann scored from the penalty spot at the end of the first half, then again in the 72nd minute on the end of a move by Paul Pogba. The Bleus' number 15 put on quite a show in the box to get past Shkodran Mustafi. A few feints then a left-footed pass parried by Manuel Neuer onto the feet of the Atlético Madrid striker. 2–0!

Paul's dream was coming true. The France team would play a home final, just as their predecessors had done in 1984 and 1998. But the hotly anticipated celebration on 10 July 2016 would end in huge disappointment. At the end of the final, lost 1–0 to Portugal thanks to a goal from Eder in extra time, Paul would lie prostrate on the pitch at the Stade de France, his first European trophy having slipped through his fingers.

Like the rest of his team, he had fallen at the final hurdle. He had not been able to provide the touch of genius the Bleus so desperately needed. 'There is always a huge amount of expectation around Paul,' commented his former manager, Pierre Mankowski. 'Then, when he's not so good, they're quick to criticise him. Sometimes we forget that he's still a very young player.'

The criticism rained down once the competition had come to an end. In France, where Paul was judged harshly, he was likened to 'an intermittent performer' who had had a nondescript tournament, to a player all too often incapable of putting his talent to the use of the team. The Italian press, despite usually praising him highly for his performances in Serie A, was also extremely tough. *La Gazzetta Dello Sport* had only seen 'the ghost' of the Juventus star during the tournament, while *La Repubblica* rubbed salt into the wounds: 'During the final, Paul Pogba missed every opportunity in a match that could have been his consecration.' Paul, who had dreamt of making the country dance while lifting the cup, finished the Euros banging his fist against the ground, frustrated by a missed opportunity.

Chapter 22

Pogback

Los Angeles, Miami, Las Vegas and New York: four weeks in the United States. To rest, have fun, enjoy life and meet lots of people. A busy and well-deserved holiday after the Euro 2016 final, a trip to be shared with millions of followers. It began on 13 July. Before setting off for America, Pogba posted a photo and a video. With the France flag wrapped around his bare back: 'Before leaving for holidays I want to share this video to show my appreciation for the amazing messages of support from the fans. Seeing how France has come together around our team is a blessing and I can't thank you enough.'

In the video Paul introduced his new 'holiday hair', platinum blond with three small *tricolore* stripes on one side. He took the opportunity to wish everyone a good holiday. But he did not stop communicating, sharing his trip step by step on Instagram and Twitter. When he was not the one showing what he was getting up to, professional or amateur paparazzi did it for him. What was certain, judging by the 39 images and videos he posted on social media, was that the French number 6 was having a good time. Meanwhile a media storm surrounding his fate was raging in Europe: would he stay at Juve? Would he go to Madrid to be coached by one of his childhood idols, Zidane? Would he choose England and United? Paul entertained himself by sending cryptic messages about his future. Seen from behind going into Hollywood's Universal Studios, *La Pioche* is holding a yellow folder captioned by his comment: 'Pogba takes his contract for a walk.' Shortly afterwards, he poses in front of the Universal globe, adding: 'Pogba medical in Universal Studios park.' As well as being caught in the company of Romelu Lukaku coming out of the 1 OAK LA nightclub in West Hollywood, the French player also had dinner with Zlatan Ibrahimović while in Los Angeles. This time it was not he who published the news; the chef Bobby Chinn posted selfies with the two footballers. Rumours immediately followed that the giant Swede, a long-time charge of Raiola, was trying to convince Paul to follow him in his new adventure at United.

From Los Angeles to Miami. *La Pioche* landed in Florida by private jet in the company of Lukaku. They planned to visit the Everglades, relax on a yacht packed with beautiful girls, shop, barbecue and shoot basketball hoops. Not to mention anyone they may or may not have planned to meet, such as Clint Capela, the Swiss basketball player with the Houston Rockets, Chad Johnson, wide receiver for the Monterrey Fundidores, or the 23 July visit by Booba, the French rapper who is a big fan of the Bleus and a friend of Karim Benzema. The most talked about photo, certainly in terms of transfer rumours, was that of 25 July: soaking in the pool with palm trees in the background, Paul is laughing heartily while next to him, with a physique that is far from athletic, stands Mino Raiola. The caption says: 'We say it all by saying nothing at all.' Could it have been any more cryptic? These nine words provoked plenty of debate and interpretation in the English and Italian press. Some believed that United were about to close the deal with Juve for £100 million. Paul also met up with his friend Antoine Griezmann in Miami. Wearing the yellow number 23 shirt of LeBron

James, the Cleveland Cavaliers wing, he went to pick him up at the airport before a kick-about in the playground and a basketball match to round off the day.

That weekend he was in Las Vegas in the company of an old friend: Uncle Pat Evra, at the Wet Republic pool party at the MGM Grand along with a hundred other revellers. Superstar DJ Calvin Harris was on the decks. There was no news about his move to United: when Andy Burton, a reporter for *Sky Sports New HQ* got close enough to ask if the agreement with United was a done deal, Pogba laconically replied: 'We'll see.' On 1 August, everyone was convinced the French player was about to fly to Manchester. But no. Here he was two days later immortalised while practising Thai boxing, and on 5 August at Madison Square Garden in New York to attend a Drake concert. Various shots of the pair followed; including one of the moment Paul gave the Canadian rapper his number 10 Juventus shirt. Some took it as a farewell gesture to the Old Lady, while others interpreted it as a last-minute change of course. But that was nothing compared to the debate generated by what Pogba posted on 28 July. At a service station on Route 66, Pogba was filling up his sports car. The photo is black and white, but his baseball cap and shoes are tinted red. Some saw it as a well-thought-out demonstration that his world was changing colour. But of course that was not an end to it; next came the rumour sparked by the selfie snapped by Jonathan Perk, a student and United fan on holiday in the United States. On 30 July, he met Paul on the streets of Los Angeles and asked him for a photo and an autograph. On his red shirt. The Frenchman agreed and gave a thumbs up.

Putting an end to this seemingly never-ending saga, wiping away false evidence, months of illusions, silence, denials and rumours came the overnight news on 9 August 2016.

At 1.21am Italian time, 0.21am English time, Manchester United pulled off a Hollywood-style move. They launched a nine-second online video with the message 'Are you ready? Pogback.' In the darkness, Paul is wearing a United sweatshirt with his hood up, *Assassin's Creed* style, without revealing his face. The traditional statement was issued at 1.35am: 'Manchester United are delighted to announce that Paul Pogba has completed his transfer from Italian club Juventus. Paul joins on a five-year contract, with the option to extend for a further year.' This launched a stream of videos, statements, declarations, comments from those involved, and United and Juve fans who were up in the middle of the night. Pogba comes out of the darkness and takes off his hood to confirm 'I'm back.' Next came the Adidas mega ad: Pogba dancing with the rapper Stormzy.

It was the Turin club who made the transfer figures official: 'Juventus Football Club S.p.A announces the agreement with Manchester United Football Club Limited for the definitive transfer of the sporting services of the footballer Paul Labile Pogba for a sum of €105 million payable in two years. The purchase value may increase by €5 million if certain conditions are met during the terms of the contract.'

Paul Pogba would earn €14 million per season for five years plus image rights, at least €5 million per year. Figures that Juventus could not afford. Mino Raiola, architect of the operation, took home an unprecedented sum. In May 2017, Football Leaks revealed that the Dutch-Italian agent had pocketed €49 million for Pogba's transfer. FIFA have opened an investigation to clarify the agent's agreements with the three parties involved. Getting back to the €105 million (£89.3 million), this was an unprecedented figure in the history of football, the highest fee ever paid for a player, prior to the transfer of Neymar Junior from Barcelona to

PSG for €222 million. This figure would provoke all kinds of comments. For the moment it was time for Paul Pogba to say goodbye and hello. The ex-number 10 would send a video message in Italian to his former fans: 'Hello everyone. It's a bit of a sad moment because I'm going to another team. It is the end of a story that started very well and I'm happy because of that. I've grown a lot and I owe Juve and you the fans a great deal. One book is closing and another is opening. I would like to thank Juventus: the footballers, fans and staff for believing in me. You will always be in my heart, thank you again, thank you for everything.' Juventus responded by publishing a video of his play and finest goals, accompanied by the hashtag #MerciPaul.

To his new fans Paul wrote: 'I am delighted to re-join United. It has always been a club with a special place in my heart and I am really looking forward to working with José Mourinho. I have thoroughly enjoyed my time at Juventus and have some fantastic memories of a great club with players that I count as friends. But I feel the time is right to go back to Old Trafford. I always enjoyed playing in front of the fans and can't wait to make my contribution to the team. This is the right club for me to achieve everything I hope to in the game.'

And to complete the picture, José Mourinho also waxed lyrical. The Portuguese manager admitted to being keen on the player back in 2015, when he was in charge at Chelsea. Back then he said of the Frenchman: 'I think everybody has an interest in Pogba. But there are things you can do and things you cannot do. I love the Eiffel Tower but I can't have the Eiffel Tower in my garden. I can't even have the Eiffel Tower of Las Vegas.' But now he did. The Americans had bought him the Eiffel Tower and he said: 'Paul will be a key part of the United team I want to build here for the future.

He is quick, strong, scores goals and reads the game better than many players much older than he is. At 23, he has the chance to make that position his own here over many years. He is young and will continue to improve; he has the chance to be at the heart of this club for the next decade and beyond.'

This brought an end to 'Pogba-day', which had begun at 1pm when the French player arrived in Manchester by private jet from Nice. He went to Carrington for the customary medical in a red and black Chevrolet Camaro kindly provided by United's sponsor General Motors.

The Red Devils brought their transfer campaign to an end that afternoon with Pogba's signing. They had certainly been busy. They had bought Zlatan Ibrahimović, Henrikh Mkhitaryan, the Armenian, from Borussia Dortmund, another Raiola player, and the Ivorian Eric Bailly. €185 million spent compared with €47 million earned through sales. Quite a transfer campaign indeed! But the richest club in the world (£515 million in revenue during the 2015–16 season according to a Deloitte report), richer than Barcelona (£463.8 million) and Real Madrid (also £463.8 million), could afford such an expensive player, as well as the most costly and controversial manager. It was not a choice sparked by the madness of bored investors, but a football business choice that was motivated by strategy, marketing and image. Strategic because it brought home the boy who, in 2012, United had allowed to slip through their fingers without earning them a penny. It put right Ferguson's worst mistake, an error that cost a four-year shortfall and money thrown away on finding someone to take the boy's place at the Academy. Motivated by image because United were demonstrating to the footballing world that they could beat off any competition, whether from Real, Barça or PSG, showing that they wanted to remain among the top clubs in world football. And after lean times during Ferguson's final years, the brief reign of David Moyes and two years under Louis van Gaal, when the fans had heard tempting names without seeing any results and dreamt of a big signing, finally the player everyone wanted had arrived. There was no need to even mention marketing, all you had to do was watch the videos or look at the windows of the Adidas shop on Manchester's Market Street to understand how much the three-striped brand had wagered on the French player in the red shirt. Juventus had done the deal of the century, just as they had in 2001 with the €147 billion lire earned from the sale of Zidane to Real Madrid, allowing them to buy almost half a team of new players. Back then they got Gigi Buffon, Pavel Nedved and Lilian Thuram; this time they acquired Gonzalo Higuaín from Napoli, as well as Miralem Pjanić, Marko Pjaca, Mehdi Benatia and Dani Alves.

And what about Paul Pogba? What did he earn from returning home? Money aside, a global profile that Juve could not give him, but United and the Premier League could. A plan that, on paper at least, could go far and bring him the Ballon d'Or he dreamt of so keenly. And who knows, perhaps also the chance to take revenge on those who, four years earlier, had not seen how much he was really worth.

Chapter 23

In the Name of the Father, in the Name of the Victims

Manchester, Sunday 21 May, 2.15pm

José Mourinho is balancing like a tightrope walker on the white line. In midfield. With his hands in his pockets, grey jumper, white shirt and black trousers, he does not look up. He is deep in thought. He comes across a loose ball. He kicks it gently, once, twice towards the net bag full of other balls. He arrives at a white right-angled line and stops. He returns to his assistants, who are overseeing the team warm-up.

Paul Pogba is to the right of the Old Trafford pitch. His long levers stretch and bend before breaking into a light run. He is preparing to pick up the ball to practise tackling, passing and the occasional shot on goal under a changing sky that is so common in this part of the world, varying the intensity of the light. Every cloud that passes has a surprise in store. Twenty minutes later the United stars return to the dressing room. The Crystal Palace team stay out on the pitch a while longer. It is the 38th and final game of the 2016–17 Premier League season, a match against the Eagles that counts for neither team. Sam Allardyce's team have pulled themselves out of the relegation quicksand thanks to an incredible end to their season. United cannot hope to finish any higher than sixth in the table, a long way behind Antonio Conte's Chelsea, the league winners, and a long way off a top-four spot that would have allowed them direct access to the Champions League. But the Special One and his team still have one last trick up their sleeves to save their season: on Wednesday 24 May, they will play Ajax in the final of the Europa League in Stockholm. Of course, newly arrived at United, Mourinho had taken home the FA Community Shield against Leicester on 7 August, and the EFL Cup against Southampton on 26 February, but these two domestic trophies cannot compare to the UEFA Cup and did not come with a Champions League place attached.

The teams are announced over the loudspeaker. Four Premier League debutants are included in the United team: Joel Pereira, aged twenty, goalkeeper; Demetri Mitchell, aged twenty, winger; Scott McTominay, aged twenty, midfielder; Josh Harrop, aged 21, midfielder. Mourinho did not follow through on his threat of a few weeks earlier (to send out the youth team in protest at such a packed fixture list) but he did pick four young players. The starting eleven, with an average age of 22, would be the youngest ever fielded by United in the Premier League. But among the debutants is Paul Pogba. Mourinho was keen to give him time on the pitch; he needed it after returning from a two match absence. His father, Antoine Fassou Pogba, had died following a long illness on 12 May at the age of 79. On Tuesday 17 May, Paul, Mathias and Florentin, alongside Antoine Fassou's other children, family members and friends, had attended his funeral. His remains, repatriated from Manchester, were buried in the Muslim section of the municipal cemetery located between Pontault-Combault and Roissy-en-Brie, where Antoine Fassou had lived for 30 years and where *La Pioche* and his brothers had grown up. The day after the ceremony, Paul paid tribute to his father on Instagram with a video: filmed at home on the sofa, Paul tried to teach his father to dab.

It was accompanied by a brief caption – 'RIP Papa' – and a heart emoji. Merci to L'Hôpital Américain de Paris and to the Christie Clinic in Manchester for all the care to my dad. *Allez Papa, c'est nous la Pogbance !!'*

Paul was welcomed with prolonged applause when he stepped out onto the Old Trafford pitch. The Reds' fans saw him as one of their own, the prodigal son returned home. They loved him. He had won so many people over, particularly the kids lining the streets around the stadium proudly wearing his number 6 red shirt. Despite that, the fans' assessments of the French player's first season at United were not conclusively positive. In the *Red News* fanzine, Sparky's 'End of Season Squad Review' claimed: 'Let's be honest, he's been a bit of disappointment, hasn't he? Not to say he won't get better, but people expecting a game-dominating monster were surely disappointed as he launched his latest dreadful 30 yard effort into the Irwell. He's a good player, may even turn out a great, but as recent leaks have shown, United were well and truly taken to the cleaners by him and his agent. He needs to realise that this isn't Serie A and he can't pose on the ball for five minutes in the middle of the park at his leisure. I'm sure he will though, I expect much more next season.' Six out of ten. A narrow margin but not too bad compared to the two slapped on Luke Shaw, the three handed to Rooney and the four dished out to Martial. But not that great either compared to the nines given to Ibra and Mata and the eight to Herrera. That United were expecting more, much more from Paul went without saying. And they were not the only ones. Frank Lampard, the former Chelsea midfielder, told *Sky Sports Monday Night Football:* 'Pogba's got fantastic attributes. He's strong, he's got great feet, he's bigger than you and he's quicker than you as a midfield player. But when you have a £90 million price tag on your shoulders, we analyse more and we want more. I'm still wondering, what's his best position? What kind of player is he? What does he want to be? I feel a little bit like he has fallen in between everything. When you pay £90 million you want to see results, and he hasn't quite delivered. He's young and he possibly will do, but as it stands he hasn't been a game-changer. The problem he has is all of our perceptions. Who would you pay £90 million or £100 million for? Suarez, Ronaldo, Messi. They bring 40 to 50 goals a season. They win games on their own week in, week out. We don't know that Paul Pogba can do that yet, but he's being judged on it.'

It did not stop there. Take Alan Shearer, former captain of England and Newcastle, who explained to *The Sun*: 'When you pay nearly £90 million for someone you would expect them to blow your mind away at times on the football pitch. But there have not been many times – if any this season – when you have watched the former Juventus midfielder and thought "wow"'.

Elderly gentlemen wearing United scarves eating pizza or a pie in the Tesco café before walking the short distance to Old Trafford will tell you the same thing. 'It's true that he hasn't really impressed us this season,' says Mark, sipping his cup of coffee. 'Let me think … Yes, perhaps his first league goal against Leicester [24 September 2016, 4–1 to the Red Devils], the home game against Southampton or Bournemouth but, to be honest, there haven't been any stand-out moments. There have been good spells, like before Christmas or January when Pogba seemed to catch fire but then it fizzled out. It hasn't been a disastrous season though.' 'Perhaps it was the price tag that did it,' interrupts Dick, munching his way through egg, sausage and beans. 'It made him a target for all the critics. United aren't winning, things aren't working, they aren't playing well? It's the fault of the £89 million French player.' This story would be repeated match after match after September 2016. Criticism from both sides of the English Channel. For example: Jamie Carragher, the former Liverpool player after the derby against Pep Guardiola's Manchester City in September (2–1 to the Citizens): 'For a central midfielder in a game of that magnitude it was one of the most ill-disciplined performances I've seen in the first 45 minutes. It was like the best kid in a school yard – he does what he wants, he runs where he wants. Forget what Pogba has cost or has done what he's done. He's not a kid.'

In early October, *France Football* put a picture of Paul in a red shirt on its cover, with the caption: 'Pogba is far off the Ballon d'Or. He is not making progress with his play. He does not make a difference in games. He is not a leader.'

Blows came from all sides, even because on 13 January 2017, he became the first Premier League footballer to have his own Twitter emoji. Any excuse was good enough. Yet, on the eve of the final league game and the Europa League final, the United faithful continued to believe in him. No one was shouting 'so much money wasted'; at most they ventured a 'come on, show us you're worth what we paid for you.' Ken, wearing a red shirt with a white collar and George Best's number 7 on his back, believes that Pogba has not been able to play at his best level because he does not have the creativity of a Pirlo or the power of a Vidal alongside him. 'The problem is that next season the Portuguese manager needs to put two strong players alongside him in midfield so he can play like he did in his last year at Juventus.' Everyone has their opinion, but all the fans have patience with the French player, giving him another chance with hope for the future.

Paul Labile Pogba did not disappoint against Crystal Palace at Old Trafford. In the fifteenth minute, he used the outside of his right foot to provide Josh Harrop with a wonderful ball. The kid from Stockport ran down the wing as if he were Cristiano Ronaldo, cut inside, got past his adversary in yellow, moved the ball from his left to his right foot and unleashed a perfect shot into the corner of the Eagles' net. He then celebrated by phoning home like ET to tell them all about it. Four minutes later and Pogba did it again. Jesse Lingard supplied *La Pioche*'s right foot in the box, and, taking advantage of a slip by Joel Ward, he slid the ball between Wayne Hennessey's legs for 2–0. The French player was jumped on by his teammates. When he freed himself from the group hug he looked up to the sky and dedicated the goal to his late father. He then tried a dance step. The fans at Old Trafford, on their feet, applauded. It was Pogba's first goal since 26 January when he scored against Hull City in the EFL Cup and his fifth in the league from 33 games played, his eighth in 50 matches. He had not had such a bad season since 2012–13. It was true that he had hit the woodwork on six occasions, but posts and crossbars do not count in football. His goal against Crystal Palace was at least one on which fans and commentators were in agreement. An ovation from the stands and an eight out of ten in the British press. It brought plenty of hope for the Stockholm final. A few seconds before the 45th minute, the French player gave up his place to Carrick. It was better not to tire him out too much before Wednesday. In the second half, Pogba stayed on the bench, dabbing. Mourinho gave Rooney a run-out in what would probably be his last game in the Theatre of Dreams after eleven years. He also sent on Angel Gomes, a promising youngster at sixteen years and 262 days. After the game there was a lap of honour for the fans. The only absentee was Mourinho, who told the *MUTV* cameras: 'Don't ask me too many things because now I'm in a final. Let me go home.'

Manchester, Monday 22 May 2017, 10.33pm

At the Manchester Arena, the curtain had just come down on a concert given by Ariana Grande, an all-American pop star beloved by teenagers. Fans, boys, girls and thousands of parent chaperones were streaming out when an explosive device went off in the foyer. The crowd poured out into the street and the neighbouring station. A long night of blood, terror and waiting began in Manchester. There was the desperate ambulance race, the cordon set up by the police, the people's solidarity, homes opened up and free taxis, the search for the missing: sons, daughters, brothers, sisters, parents who had disappeared after the explosion. Then came confirmation from the police: it was an act of terrorism. The first reports of the attack spoke of nineteen victims and 50 injured. In the end the death toll would rise to 22, with 59 injured; so many lives cut short, children, teenagers, young people. A massacre, the worst in the United Kingdom since the 2005 London bombings.

Manchester, Tuesday 23 May 2017

Manchester was a city in mourning and under siege. Ariana Grande's trademark bunny ears headband became a black ribbon, a symbol of the mourning. Dozens of police officers combed the city in search of the attacker's possible accomplices. Salman Abedi, aged 23, a Briton of Libyan origin, was the suicide bomber who had blown himself up in the Manchester Arena. The massacre was claimed by so-called Islamic State. Messages of grief arrived from around the world, while Manchester came together around the victims and the injured. In Albert Square flowers, candles and thousands of people amassed for a vigil. The city's two teams also took part in the mourning and offered their help. Manchester City tweeted: 'It's with great sadness we hear of the terrible events at the Arena. Our hearts go out to all affected and to our city's emergency services.' Guardiola, manager of the Citizens, said: 'Shocked. Can't believe what happened last night. My deepest condolences to the families and friends of the victims. #Ilovemanchester' His wife and two daughters had been at the Manchester Arena.

At Carrington, United observed a minute's silence before training. The players took to Twitter to voice their thoughts: Wayne Rooney, the captain, wrote. 'Devastating news this morning. Thoughts and prayers are with all those affected.' Paul Pogba posted 'Peace', followed by these words: 'My condolences to all families of the victims in Manchester and to all families who are losing loved ones in so many countries due to acts of violence.' Messages of solidarity also flooded in from former players such as Éric Cantona, David Beckham and Cristiano Ronaldo. UEFA agreed to the request to cancel United's pre-final press conference. Mourinho's words of condolence came through the club website: 'We're all very sad about the tragic events. We can't take out of our minds and hearts the victims and their families. I know, even during my short time here, that the people of Manchester will pull together as one. We have a job to do and will fly to Sweden to do that job. It's a pity we cannot fly with the happiness we always have before a big game.'

Stockholm, Friends Arena, Wednesday 24 May 2017, 10.39pm

At the final whistle, José Mourinho turned towards the press gallery, shouted and stuck up his index finger. He was telling everybody he was the number one. Celebrating with clenched fists, his face lit up and he jumped into the arms of a boy wearing a red sweatshirt. The two fell to the ground and rolled on the grass, getting up and jumping in the air together. Mourinho celebrated the victory over Ajax in the final with his son, José Junior. In game number 64 of his first season at United, the Special One secured the only trophy missing from the Old Trafford cabinet. He had saved what had been a terrible league season by winning a European trophy that the greats, and he himself, had always snubbed, but that admitted United to the Champions League. He had won a different kind of treble (UEFA Cup, Community Shield, EFL CUP) after his 2010 treble with Inter. In his own way and with his own style, not much poetry but a lot of prose, not always of the highest quality. He was once again the king of cups: of fourteen finals played he had won twelve. It was the latest title to add to his personal collection of 25. It was a title that looked a lot like redemption for the Portuguese manager. Finally, after months and months of angry, long faces, he was smiling and jumping around like a madman amidst the celebrations.

At the final whistle, Paul Pogba went over to the fans on his own and performed the 'Billy Dance', his new victory celebration in place of the Dab; it was borrowed from Billax, one of his childhood friends. After losing two finals (the Champions League 2015 with Juve against Barcelona and the Euro 2016 final with the Bleus against Portugal), the French player had won his first European title. But above all he had been convincing. This time he had lived up to expectations, responding to Mourinho, his teammates, the fans and his critics. This time the £89-million man had made the difference. It was obvious immediately that it would be his night. Twenty-two seconds after the kick-off, United lobbed the ball into the Dutch area. André Onana, the Dutch keeper, came off his line and almost slammed into his teammate Joël Veltman. The ball flew off; a Dutch defender managed somehow to get it away but it ended up near Paul, who stopped the ball with his chest and shot on the volley with his right foot. The result went just wide. But it was a demonstration that the player was ready to give his all. That night in Sweden began with what was supposed to be a minute's silence in honour of the victims of the Manchester attack. Players wearing both red and white and red and blue shirts with black armbands lined up facing one another in the centre circle as the stands fell silent. But the silence quickly became applause, a cry of pride, of defiance: 'Manchester! Manchester!' 'Come on United, do it for Manchester,' read a card held up by a spectator; 'United against terrorism' read a banner behind Sergio Romero's goal. There were plenty of messages remembering the victims of the attack, even if on such an emotional night there was also the odd stadium prank, such as the banner that read 'Zlatan, stay and you can shag my wife.' Speaking of Ibrahimović – dressed in black and on crutches, he would appear at the end of the game to celebrate the win with his teammates. A win that had plenty to do with the number 6. In front of the defence, alongside Marouane Fellaini, Paul dominated every part of the pitch. He swept up dangerous balls in the midfield, won the duel with Davy Klassen, the Ajax captain, and sent Marcus Rashford into orbit. For once, it was a dream night for the new midfielder, the box-to-box man. He showed this in the eighteenth minute of the first half when he gave his team the advantage. United picked up the ball to the right of the Dutch goal; Mata supplied Fellaini, who picked out Pogba on the edge of the area. The Frenchman rediscovered Pogboom and unleashed a bullet with his left foot. The shot took a deflection off the leg of Davinson Sánchez, the twenty-year-old Colombian centre-back. The ball reared up, flew off in an unpredictable direction and there was nothing poor Onana could do. It was certainly a lucky goal but

well-deserved given how Pogba had played and would continue to play over 94 minutes. After seeing the ball hit the
back of the net, Paul ran away like a madman; Darmian and
Mkhitaryan were the first to reach him and hug him. When
he broke free, he looked up and pointed to the sky in tribute
to his father. It was a goal of redemption, both for him and
Mourinho, confirming that he was worth spending so much
on. It was a response to Matthijs de Ligt, the Ajax defender,
who had said the day before the final, echoing the words of
Johan Cruyff: 'I've never seen a bag of money score a goal.'
Goals in two consecutive matches for the first time since he
had arrived in Manchester. It was an extremely important
goal as far as the Special One's plans were concerned. The
Portuguese manager had set up a barrier, or even better a
trap in the midfield to stop the young Dutch players, giving Paul the opportunity to play in the way that suited him
best. He allowed a young Ajax team (with an average age
of 22) to delude themselves, occupying the midfield, keeping the ball (69 per cent possession) and giving United the
chance to win. Ajax's young players had talent and plenty of
good intentions; their passing was attractive and they played
well, but there was no bite to their game. So much so that
Sergio Romero had a relaxing evening in goal. There was
no danger. The same could not be said of Onana, who had
to pick the ball out of the back of his net for a second time
in the 47th minute. After a corner from Mata, Fellaini kept
the Dutch centre-backs busy while Smalling jumped higher
than Joël Veltman, heading the ball into the ground. With
his back to goal, body to body with the Dutch defender,
Mkhitaryan picked up the ball and scorpion-kicked it into
the net, surprising everyone. It was 2–0. Mourinho's strategy
had worked: his 4–1–4–1 formation had beaten the Dutch
manager Peter Bosz's 4–3–3. From then on the game was

over. José even allowed himself the luxury of sending Rooney on with the captain's armband just before the referee blew the final whistle. After that it was all joy, celebrations and dedications: 'We know things like this [the terror attack at Manchester Arena] are very sad, all over the world not only in Manchester, in London, in Paris,' said a bare-chested Paul Pogba, 'so we had to focus because it was a very important game. We won for Manchester, we won for the people who died.'

Acknowledgements

We would like to thank the following people for their recollections and collaboration: Stéphane Albe, Pascal Antonetti, Sébastien Barniaud, Christian Bassila, Gérard Bonneau, Habib Bouacida, Razik Brikh, Michael Bunel, Vincent Cabin, Alexandre Corboz, Carol Dalby, Paul Dalby, Jean-Pierre Damont, Jean-Paul Delahaye, Fabiana Della Valle, Mamadou Diouf, Benoît Donkele, Vincent Duluc, Guy Ferrier, Michele Fornasier, Jérémy Frick, David Frio, Emanuele Gamba, Paolo Garimberti, Mamadou Konte, Michael Le Baillif, William Le Pogam, Frédéric Lipka, Yoan Loche, Jean-Pierre Louvel, Johann Louvel, Paul McGuinness, Mamadou Magassa, Pierre Mankowski, Yves Martin, Florian Maurice, André Merelle, Pierre Michaud, Alain Olio, Davide Petrucci, James Robson, François Rodrigues, Franck Salle, Naby Sarr, Bruno Satin, Patrick Sembla, Julien Sokol, Nicolas Soussan, Jérémie Sutter, Sambou Tati, Ounoussou Timera, Alban Traquet, Guido Vaciago, Javier Villagarcía and Ali Zarrak.

Thank you to Michael Sells, Duncan Heath, Philip Cotterell, Laura Bennett, Laure Merle d'Aubigné and Roberto Domínguez.

Thanks to Elvira, Céline, Lorenzo, Mathieu and Olmo for their support and valuable advice.

Dedicated to the victims of the Manchester Arena attack.

Finally, happy reading to Elisa, Méline, Laure, Arthur, Jules, Colin, Tom, Louis and Noah.